RABINDRANATH TAGORE
AMONG SAINTS

Bipul Kumar Gangopadhyay

Translated by

Swaraj Kumar Chakrabarti
Dr Amitava Sanyal

Vitasta

Published by
Renu Kaul Verma
Vitasta Publishing Pvt Ltd
4348/4C, Ansari Road, Daryaganj
New Delhi-110 002
info@vitastapublishing.com

ISBN: 978-81-19670-89-5
English Translation
© Swaraj Kumar and Dr Amitava Sanyal
First Edition 2024

MRP ₹395

The Publisher and Translators gratefully acknowledge all Open Source pictures available in the worldwide web, Creative Commons, Google sources and Wikimedia used in this work of non-fiction.

Editor: Soumitro Das
Layout and Cover Design by Rohit Gautam
Printed by Chaman Enterprises, New Delhi

CONTENTS

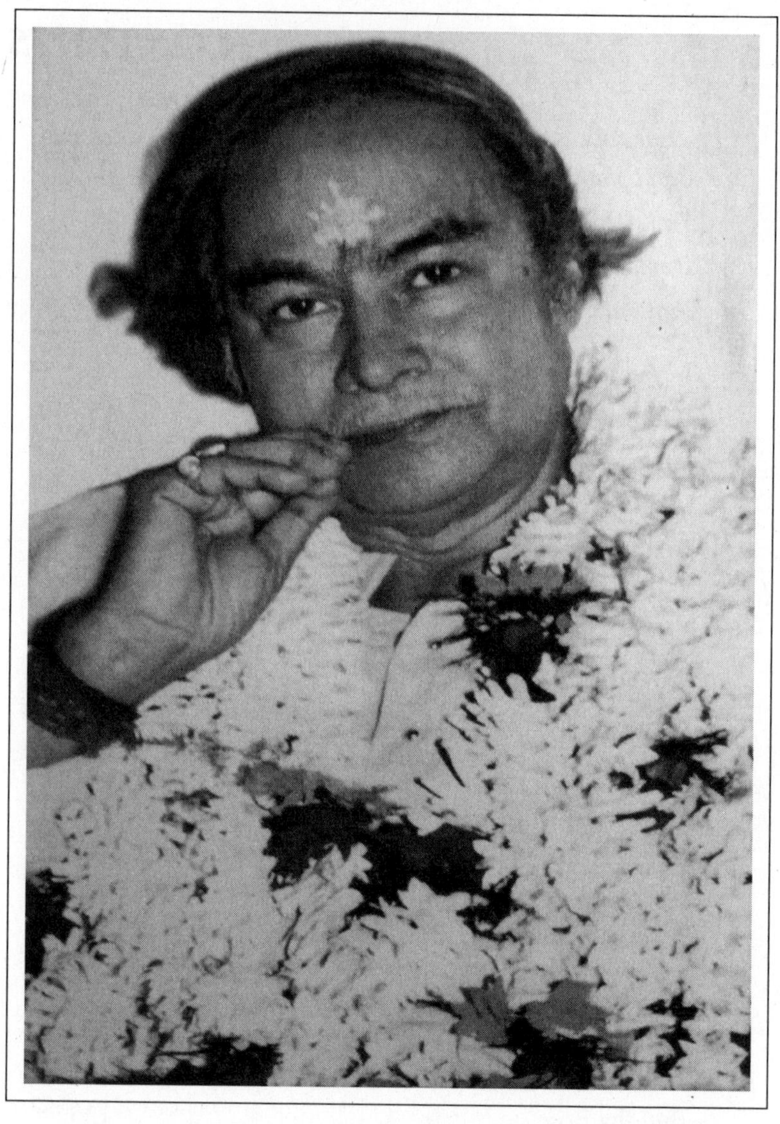

AUTHOR
BIPUL KUMAR GANGOPADHYAY

BIPUL KUMAR GANGOPADHYAY

He is a well-recognised name in India's spiritual world and literature. He was born on 1 September 1935, at the auspicious hour early before sunrise (Brahmo Muhurta) in an enlightened Brahmin family. In this family, four siddha (reached enlightenment) great saints were born. Amongst them are, Sri Sri Loknath Brahmachari, Sri Sri Madhabananda Giri's Gurudeb (master) - Mahayogi and Maha gyani Sri Sri Bhagaban Gangopadhyay.

He is the youngest son of a religious father Sri Digindra Kumar Gangopadhyay and a religious Mahasadhika mother Nibedita Debi. At the tender age of nine (1944), he was initiated by Sri Sri Ramthakur in Dhaka city (now in Bangladesh). From the age of ten, he started writing poems. At that time, he was a student at Dhaka's Ramkrishna Mission school. At the age of twelve, he wrote the Ramayana in a poetic form.

During his student life, while studying Bengali Honours, he became famous as a poet, writer, and editor of the *Smriti Patrika*. One day he had a sudden glimpse of universal consciousness. For three days he was self-buried in deep contemplation. In 1961 his first written play Tathokim received the first prize as a one-act play during Tagore's centennial celebration. He also started becoming famous as the editor of *Anandam Patrika*.

His next written book was *Creator knows his creation is not eternal.* This book received accolades from Bengal's distinguished poets, learned people and newspapers. His next book *Going and will go on* comprising of four one-act plays was broadcast on the radio, played on the stage, and received much popularity. At the same time, his edited magazine *The Nectar of Pain* (published in Bengali, English and German languages) received fame nationally and internationally.

His life changed dramatically in 1969 when he visited India's oldest Tantric place – the abode of Mahasatipith at Tarapith, Birbhum, West Bengal. For the next twenty-five years, he wrote five volumes of what eventually became the book *Mahapith Tarapith* and received international acclaim. This voluminous creation fetched him many awards from saints, learned people and newspapers. His book in Bengali *Sadhu Sannidhey Rabindranath* (*Rabindranath Tagore among Saints*) received tremendous accolades immediately after its publication.

TRANSLATORS

Swaraj Kumar Chakrabarti, a retired Chemical Engineer from Ohio EPA (Environmental Protection Agency), USA has had a deep connection with literature (both in English and in Bengali) from childhood. He has been a frequent contributor to *Amritam* magazine published by Bipul Kumar Gangopadhyay, Kolkata. He was the chairman of the North America Bangamela conference and is an active member and past President of Central Ohio Bengali Cultural Association. He has written small articles throughout his life, and he plans to put them together so that a book can be published. He is, along with Dr Amitava Sanyal, the English translator of Bipul Kumar Gangopadhyay's book *Sadhu Sannidhey Rabindranath.* Since he is passionate about Rabindra and Nazrul, he has produced the documentary Achena Ajana Rabindra o Nazrul.

Dr Amitava Sanyal, PhD (Pharmacy), MBA, has worked in the pharmaceutical industry both in India and in the USA in senior management positions. He retired from Abbott Laboratories, USA in 2013, after 36 years. Since childhood he has been an ardent fan of Swami Vivekananda, Netaji Subhas Chandra Bose, and Rabindranath Tagore, and enjoyed reading all available information on them. He played an active role as Secretary of the Science Club, Kolkata and as founder member of Central Ohio Bengali Cultural Association, had organised several charitable, cultural, and educational events. He came in contact with the spiritual writer Sri Bipul Kumar Gangopadhya in 1999 and was very impressed by his books, from which he found lots of unknown information about his heroes. At Bipulda's request he agreed to translate the book on *Rabindranath Tagore among Saints,* jointly with Swaraj Chakrabarti.

PREFACE

Sadhu Sannidhey Rabindranath

We translated the book into English language so that Tagore could be discovered in a new dimension across the world. He received the Nobel Prize as a poet, but why he became famous and was recognised as a world poet is not understood by many readers. It is because his writing connected humanity at large. The secret lies in Tagore's extraordinary mind and his universal consciousness. He reached this mental state by spiritually enriching himself all his life and never making it public. The enrichment came from his lifelong contacts with the sages of India. He, therefore, was a poet nurtured behind the scenes by spiritual bliss.

Representing the true reflection of India's soul, Tagore's writing not only reached every category of humanity, but it also embraced the world. That is the uniqueness of his genius. The following example illustrates his philosophy.

Once Albert Einstein was asked about the most powerful and important phenomenon in his life. After thinking for a while, he said 'compound interest'. A small deposit of funds growing several times with time without any further investment simply by the miracle of compound interest overwhelmed Einstein's mind.

Though Tagore was never asked this question, his researchers know for sure how he would have responded. 'Freedom of mind' would have been his stoic answer. Tagore always called it *Sarbanuvuti meaning 'feeling your presence everywhere in the universe. This is quite consistent with India's core philosophy - Vasudhaiva Kutumbakam* (The world is one family). Tagore said. 'My freedom is in the light of the sky, my freedom is in the dust, in the grass. My liberation is in the universal mind'. This universal consciousness of his mind was manifested in his songs, writings and touched the hearts of humanity.

The original author Bipul Kumar Gangopadhyay, himself a *Kriyayogi* expert, an author and highly spiritual personality, painstakingly met and interviewed those Himalayan yogis who had interactions with Tagore privately. Interviewing them, he could get a glimpse into Tagore's mind. Tagore kept these interactions completely private during his lifetime.

It has been our humble effort to translate for the first time into English, experiences Tagore had with nineteen sages. We will consider ourselves blessed if readers find this translation enlightening about Tagore who represents India's soul and was referred to as Gurudev by Mahatma Gandhi.

Amitava Sanyal and Swaraj Chakrabarti

Columbus, Ohio, USA

25 September 2023

INTRODUCTION

THE BOOK *Rabindranath Tagore among Saints* unfolds the unknown aspect of deep spirituality of the sage poet Rabindranath.

Throughout his life Rabindranath, always in search of meeting monks, came into contact with many saints. However, he kept this valuable experience to himself and didn't publicise it.

He thoroughly and silently relished this stream of nectar in his own mind.

That is why this side of his spirituality, meaningful as it was, remained unknown to Rabindra researchers. But God decided otherwise. The determination, born out of an unknown force, resulted in the writing of this book. The author is convinced that this book will be a memorable present to the lovers of Rabindranath.

It is expected that, by reading this book, kindhearted readers will gain an insight into a new and unknown facet of Rabindranath's remarkable life. Let me first explain how strangely I got inspired to write this book.

I got the inspiration to write this book in 1974, in the course of my first visit to Mahayogi Bahera Baba. After that initial visit and for six long years, I was blessed by his company. Bahera Baba was the yogi guru of Maharshi Debendranath Tagore, father of Rabindranath Tagore. Bahera Baba, at the earnest invitation of Debendranath, attended Rabindranath's marriage (9 December 1884) ceremony at Jorasanko Thakur Bari, and blessed the newlywed couple. Many members of the Tagore family were given yoga lessons by Bahera Baba, at the request of Debendranath. More than 200 years old at the time of my first visit to him, Bahera Baba, who achieved Yoga Siddhi at Himalaya's Gyanganj, related these unpublished facts to me.

I have been a witness to his yogic power several times. All classes of people from West Bengal have been blessed by Bahera Baba. Every year, he used to come to Kolkata and stay for a month. Everyday hundreds of people used to come to him with their problems. He used to resolve their sufferings by excercising his yogic supernatural power. Whosoever came to see him, like a seer of truth, this great man could see the past, present, and future of that person and relate that to him or her instantly. On occasions, without being asked, Bahera Baba could tell what the enquirer had in his or her mind and address it. All that Baba needed was a look at that person. Over a long spell of fifty years, he had blessed all sections of people. Those who had witnessed him for fifty years, from their childhood, confessed to seeing not a speck of physical change in Baba. While Baba maintained the same physical look, the devotees aged during these fifty years. Baba used to stay every year at Ballygunge Place, Kolkata.

I am a witness to his numerous acts of supernatural power. In the second of my five-volume book *Mahapith Tarapith*, I have recounted exhaustively with pictures about Baba's divine life story. It took me twenty-five years (1969-1994) to write my five-volume book. Whatever predictions Baba made about me when I first met him in 1974, came true. This ancient Mahayogi always used to call me endearingly as 'Yogibaba'.

My second and third inspirations for this book on Rabindranath came from my senior gurubhai Jatindra Mohan Dasgupta (JM Dasgupta) and yogiraj Ramnath Aghori Baba.

Dr JM Dasgupta was the family physician. Rabindranath had a long and deep relationship with JM Dasgupta. Rabindranath had an earnest desire to meet JM Dasgupta's Gurudev, the sage famous all over the country, Sri Sri Ramthakur. However, due to lack of time and coordination that meeting never took place.

On Rabindranath's earnest request, a disciple of Sri Sri Bamakyapa introduced him to Yogiraj Ramnath Aghoribaba.

Rabindranath was highly impressed after conversing with Aghoribaba and witnessing his yogic power. Yogiraj Aghoribaba informed me about unpublished incidents relating to Rabindranath. I have had the good fortune of enjoying the divine companionship of Aghoribaba for five long years (1974-1979). I described his divine life in the second volume of my book *Mahapith Tarapith*. In 1980 at the age of 135 Aghoribaba passed away in Kolkata.

It was while writing *Mahapith Tarapith*, that I gathered much information about Rabindranath.

Besides this, I came to know many facts about Rabindranath from reading the great life stories of Ramananda Bharati, Brahmabandab Upadhyay, Yogacharya Bhupendranath Sanyal, world famous *Kriyayogi* Buddha Bose, Mahatma Bijoy Krishna Goswami, Rishi Aurobindo, Bhagini Nivedita, and Mahasadhika Rangama.

Earlier (from 1965 to 1968), I heard many unknown facts about Rabindranath from Hemlata Tagore (affectionately blessed by Rabindranath), Dr Radhakamal Mukhopadhyay, Dilip Kumar Roy, Rajarao Dhirendra Narayan Roy, and Soumendranath Tagore. They had all closely observed Rabindranath for a long time. They shared both good and bad times of Rabindranath on the same platform. I received from them many unknown facts about the domestic life of Rabindranath. I have published those in my magazine *Amritam* in a series of articles.

Before I describe in detail the above five famous spiritual personalities, I need to mention something else here. Besides gathering information from the above-mentioned Mahayogi and learned thinkers, I have added more information for a good length of time, from other life stories of spiritual leaders, contemporary books, and magazines *(like Banga Darshan, Probasi Bharat Barsha, Bichitra, Bharati, Modern Review, Sanjibani, Tattobodhini etc)*, Rabindranath's writings, Gitabitan, letters, and Brahmo Sangeet.

The database at the end of this book gives a summary of this information. Having received an unknown heavenly instruction, I have put together this information and that resulted in the birth of the book *Rabindranath Tagore among Saints*.

While writing this book, the person who sincerely assisted me most is Srijukta Hemlata Tagore (1873-1967), dearly blessed by Rabindranath. She was the elder daughter-in-law of Rabindranath's elder brother Dwijendranath Tagore. She was also Raja Ram Mohan Roy's great-great-granddaughter.

Due to this relationship, she was referred to as a bridge of hundred years between Raja Ram Mohan and Rabindranath. She was well known in Santiniketan as *Baroma*.

Stalwarts like Pandit Jawaharlal Nehru, Dr Bidhan Chandra Roy and others gave due respect to her, befitting her name Baroma (elder mother). Hemlata Tagore observed the world poet Rabindranath from a very close distance for a long time. In the year 1965, while residing in Puri, this great lady at the age of 92 blessed me with many unknown incidents from the life of Rabindranath. Day after day, while ruminating on the past, she conveyed to me facts otherwise unknown to the public. Especially, she had lots to say about Swami Vivekananda, her husband's classmate, and friend. She revealed to me a treasure trove of information about contacts between Vivekananda and Rabindranath, contacts that remained unrecounted outside the family. She gifted to me her collection of poems called *Alor Pakhi* (radiant bird) . It is therefore absolutely appropriate that I gratefully dedicated the book *Rabindranath Tagore among Saints* to her.

Rabindranath visited and stayed for a while in the house of his close associate Dr Radhakamal Mukhopadhyay, vice chancellor of Lucknow University, chairman of India's planning commission and internationally famous economist. The character of the professor in the play *Raktakarobi* written by Rabindranath is based on Dr Radhakamal Mukhopadhyay. The latter spoke to me about informal conversations that he had had with Rabindranath. Being the leader amongst expatriate Bengalis, Radhakamal hosted in his house besides

Rabindranath, Pandit Jawaharlal Nehru, Netaji Subhas Chandra Bose, Atul Prasad Sen and Dilip Kumar Roy. These great people came many times to his place and stayed.

Over a period of time (1965-1970), while staying at his home in Puri, he apprised me of many unknown facts about Rabindranath. I will remain grateful to him for this.

Rabindranath loved the songs of Dilip Kumar Roy, son of Dwijendra Lal Roy who was a literary critic of Rabindranath. Many times, Rabindranath invited Dilip Kumar Roy to Jorasanko and Santiniketan and listened with pleasure to his songs. Rabindranath used to fondly call Dilip Kumar Roy, Mantu, his nickname.

The king of Lalgola, Rajarao Dhirendra Narayan Roy, a close friend of Dilip Kumar Roy, was also dear to Rabindranath. He started learning recitation during his adolescence by sitting in the lap of Rabindranath. His maternal grandfather was Acharya Ramendrasundar, who was very close to Rabindranath. Rajarao Dhirendranarayan observed Rabindranath from close quarters. He described his experience (1968-1971) in detail to this writer.

Rabindranath's very dear nephew Soumendranath Tagore, a good writer and orator, informed this writer about different facets of Rabindranath's life. He informed this writer about Hemlata Tagore. He performed the last rites of Baroma in Puri when she expired (1967), nearly hundred years old. Hemlata Tagore had no children. The writer is immensely grateful to Hemlata Tagore, Radhakamal Mukhopadhyay, Dilip Kumar Roy, Soumendranath Tagore and Rajarao Dhirendranath Roy for sharing with me their experiences with Rabindranath.

The writer is indebted to Baul expert Purna Das Baul, son of Khyapa Baul Nabani Das. Purna Das Baul enriched this writer with stories of his father's presentation of Baul songs to Rabindranath and their spiritual conversation.

The writer is grateful to Ruma Devi, worthy disciple of world famous *Kriyayogi* Buddhadeb Bose. One needs to mention here with special reference to Ruma Devi's maternal uncle, internationally known yoga expert Biswanath Ghosh. I have explained about Biswanath Ghosh, supernaturally blessed son of universal mother Tarama, in my fifth volume of the book *Mahapith Tarapith*. The writer expresses his deep gratitude to Biswanath Ghosh for introducing him to his niece Ruma Devi.

In addition, the writer is indebted to Tapas Dev, distinguished *Kriyayogi* and director of the Yoga Cure Center at Behala, Kolkata.

The writer is ever grateful to the ex-registrar of Bolpur sub-registry office and reputed writer Sri Chittapriya Mitra. With written proof, he showed this writer, how lord S P Sinha sold for one rupee the plot at Bolpur, to Maharshi Debendranath Tagore on which Santiniketan was to eventually come up. On this matter, the writer is also grateful to Professor Satya Prakash Chakrabarti and his friend Krishna Gopal Ghosh.

Professor Soma Chakrabarti a great lover of Rabindra sangeet and spiritual lady, has greatly contributed towards the reporting of the role music played in the spiritual development of Rabindranath.

Assistance has been provided by Shibotosh Majumder, Himangshu Mukhopadhyay and reputed writer Tarashish

Gangopadhyay. All the above-mentioned are very dear to me and therefore expressing gratitude will be redundant. They have my blessings, may they grow and prosper.

My long-standing effort will come to fruition if my kind readers find peace and joy after reading this book *Rabindranath Tagore among saints*. It is because peace and love are the forerunners to the realisation of God.

Sage poet Rabindranath was the ultimate worshiper of joy and peace. The spiritual companionship of saints has been a representation of his quest for eternal joy and lasting peace. He tasted the nectar of joy and peace. Sitting on the shore of the stream of nectar, the great poet witnessed in ecstasy that a 'wave of joy is filling the universe'.

Happiness is traversing all around—from sky, air, water, fire, universe to every living being continuously. This is happening because joy is the reflection of our soul. This everlasting soulful joy is the source of our birth, of the stability in our lives, and its final ending. Though joy blends with the earth at the end, it is indestructible. Joy is therefore an all-pervading divine soul; it is the soul uniting with the supreme spirit.

IN THE NAME OF
THE FATHER

RABINDRANATH TAGORE, during his lifetime, came into divine contact with many saints belonging to different religious beliefs. The spiritual nature of Maharshi Debendranath and the rich heritage in literature, culture, and music of the Tagore family, influenced Rabindranath to become attracted towards *sadhus*. Above all, his inborn spiritual nature, search for the inner self, and broad outlook made him seek the company of saints. His spiritual consciousness can be traced back to his childhood.

Maharshi Debendranath, though a family person, was a devotee of the Brahmo religion and leader of the Brahmo Samaj. He enriched his life with the idealism of the Upanishads. He, therefore, gradually reared his youngest son, Rabindranath, as a devotee to the joyful nectar of the Upanishadic Brahma. Maharshi Debendranath was very fortunate because he met holy persons not only at home and in different parts of the country, such as the Himalayas, but also in China which he visited in 1875. He received the blessings of well-known saints such as Ramkrishna Paramahansa and from Bamakhyapa at Tarapith, Birbhum. In addition to meeting several saints during his travels in the Himalayas, Maharshi Debendranath had the rare opportunity to come into contact with Mahayogi Bahera Baba from Gyanganj situated high up deep in the Himalayas.

MAHARSHI DEBENDRANATH TAGORE

During his later years, he received spiritual discourses at his residence from famous saints of different religious sects (Sakta, Baishnav, Shaiva, Vedantic, *Kriyayogi* etc) like Ramananda Bharati, Bijoykrishna Goswami, Narendranath Dutta (later Swami Vivekananda) and Yogi Bhupendranath Sanyal. Despite differences in opinion and ideologies, Rabindranath had a pleasant relationship with all of these pious people.

From the dawn of life till his twilight years, Rabindranath maintained the tradition of close contact with sadhus.

Rabindranath, however, kept this spiritual side of his life to himself only. It is as if his flood of writings stopped at the shore of the ocean of spirituality.

Maharshi Debendranath had a profound spiritual influence on Rabindranath. Rabindranath was the youngest son of his father. Maharshi Deb was middle aged when Rabindranath was born. Debendranath was born on 17 May 1817. His father Prince Dwarkanath Tagore, architect of modern India, was a close well-wisher of Raja Ram Mohan Roy. Based on this relationship, Debendranath came into close contact with Raja Ram Mohan Roy. He gradually developed an attraction towards worshipping formless, undifferentiated Brahma and at the age of 26, was initiated into the Brahmo religion by Ramchandra Bidyabagish.

Within three years of this, at the mere age of 19, he lost his father. Thereafter, he had to keep a tight grip over his finances and subject his family to considerable hardship in order to repay the huge debt his father had incurred. For this great self-sacrifice, he earned the title *Maharshi*. Subsequently, he became busy with the establishment of the Brahmo Samaj, writing books and travelling in the Himalayas.

At the age of 44, (1861), his youngest son, Rabindranath, was born on 7 May 1861. Maharshideb, at age 55, and guided by an inspiration of divine origin, established Brahmacharya Ashram at Santiniketan on 22 December 1872.

The source of that inspiration was Mahatantrik Sri Sri Bamakhyapa of Tarapith

At the age of 56, on an early morning, the *Maharshi*, at the invitation of his friend, Lord S P Sinha, was travelling from Bolpur to Raipur. On his way, he unexpectedly heard from locals about Sri Sri Bamakhyapa, the powerful Tantric and worshipper of goddess Tara at the famous shrine of Tarapith, whose name had spread all over Birbhum. What he heard encouraged him to meet with this famous saint. With great difficulty, after walking several miles from Mollarpur, he managed to reach the Tarapith cremation ground, surrounded by dense forests. He found the great Bamakhyapa, sitting in deep contemplation, at the feet of the shrine of the Goddess. In 1868, the Maharshi had the opportunity to meet in his home at Jorasanko, Calcutta, Ramkrishna Paramahansa, the embodiment of the self-existing spirit. This time, he saw and was visibly moved by the spiritually radiant, blood shot eyes of this huge dark-skinned figure of Bamakhyapa. They gazed at each other for some time and then Bamakhyapa asked about the reason for the Maharshi's visit.

The Maharshi replied with deep reverence, that the purpose of the visit was only to see him and not for any worldly interests. Bamakhyapa was pleased to hear this; it spoke of the *Maharshi's* detached approach to things spiritual. Then he said to the *Maharshi* 'You are on your way to Raipur to keep the invitation of Sinha's house. On your path, you will see a big plot of land, in the middle of which there will be a big chatim tree. Meditate under the tree. You will find peace by realising the self-luminous soul inside. You build your ashram right there. With the blessings of Tarama, you will unexpectedly get possession of the land for your ashram.'

The *Maharshi* was surprised at this unexpected revelation, and his respect for this all- knowing, all -seeing seer became even greater. Upon instruction from Bamakhyapa, he visited Tarama's temple. The *Maharshi*, though a worshipper of formless, unconditioned Brahma, was not disrespectful of the divine form of Brahma.

His father, prince Dwarkanath Tagore, used to celebrate Durga Puja with great splendor at his Jorasanko residence. Young Debendranath, not only participated in the Durga Puja, but also, at his father's request, invited his father's friend, the great reformer Raja Ram Mohan Roy, who respectfully accepted the offerings from Ma Durga.

After seeing the beautiful idol of Tarama, he happily accepted, at the request of the temple priests, the mid-day *mahaprasad* offered to Tarama. It was customary for the priests to offer *prasad* made with rice to any saint or guest visiting Tarama during noon time. This was the instruction to the servers at the temple from the Maharani Rani Bhavani of Natore. The temple was situated under the jurisdiction of this kingdom. For hundreds of years, this practice had been kept alive by the descendants of the King's family.

After accepting the *mahaprasad* from Tarama's temple, he returned to Bamakhyapa and received his blessings before returning to Bolpur.

During his journey to Raipur, he did find the big chatim tree as described by Bamakhyapa. As instructed, he went into deep meditation under the tree. After a long time under meditation, he suddenly realised divine pleasure and resplendency. Seeing Bamakhyapa's prediction coming true, he felt immensely pleased. He decided to build his ashram at this sacred spot.

With his mind made up, he visited his friend Lord S P Sinha and requested the zamindar to sell him the plot on which the chatim tree stood. Lord Sinha gladly agreed to the request but did not wish to take any money since this was for a noble cause. In fame and fortune Debendranath was worth as much as Lord Sinha. He therefore said, 'You must take money from me because I will not take the land without paying the price.'

Lord Sinha smiled and then said 'Okay, whatever money I will demand, you will need to pay. Do you agree?' Debendranath agreed.

After a few days, they both reached Bolpur registry office at noon. Though the *Maharshi* brought hundreds of rupees with him for the price of the land, Lord Sinha, to the *Maharshi's* astonishment, asked for only one rupee and sold the land to Debendranath. The registrar and the assistants were equally surprised at this magnanimous gesture of Lord Sinha.

After the land registration was completed, a shocked

Maharshi said to Lord Sinha 'I have been defeated by your greatness.' Lord Sinha replied, 'There is no greatness. I am contributing to a noble cause espoused by a friend.'

Debendranath told Lord Sinha about how every prediction of Bamakhyapa, including the one related to the acquisition of the land, had come true. Lord Sinha said, 'I have heard about this great saint. I haven't been fortunate yet to meet him. I have a great desire to meet him given the time and the opportunity.' In 1872, at the age of 55, the *Maharshi* established this Brahmacharya ashram under the chatim tree and experienced the inner peace and tranquility predicted by Bamakhyapa.

Rabindranath was only an 11-year-old boy at that time. He was the one, having the divine power within himself, who continued his father's spiritual legacy by expanding and bringing Santiniketan to worldwide recognition.

Rabindranath was fortunate, though he was the middle-aged Maharshi's youngest son, to have enjoyed the sacred company of his father for 44 years until Maharshi passed away on 20 January 1905 at the age of 88 years. Rabindranath's spiritual journey was vastly influenced by his long association (more than half his life) with his father at home, in journey through the Himalayas, attending Brahmo Samaj gatherings, and by meeting many saints of his time.

Rabindranath documented his love and reverence for his father in his autobiography *Jeevan Smriti*. The spiritual longing to seek out the company of saints started from his childhood in the presence of his father and continued throughout his youth and adult life. Let us analyse how, moved by some unfathomable factors, his spiritual development started and flourished under a very conducive environment while he was growing up.

His *upanayana* (thread ceremony) happened at a tender age of only 10 years. Head shaven, this young boy while chanting the Gayatri mantra in the sacred early dawn hour (when the mind and the body remain in unison), felt the happy reverberations of the universe.

Thereafter, at Santiniketan, and during his trips to the Himalayas with his father, he routinely got up early in the morning and recited the *slokas* from Bhagavad Gita and the Upanishads.

Listening to *slokas*, his father's self-immersed meditative image left an indelible impression in his mind which he mentioned many times in his autobiography (*Jeevan Smriti*). This sacred experience led Rabindranath to develop a universal consciousness and the unison of his soul with the supreme spirit. That is why the young poet wrote 'My earthly eyes fail to notice you because you permeate the very sense of my vision.' This universal consciousness later helped Rabindranath, even as a young man, to situate himself in an all-pervasive universe and have a glimpse of the undefined creator Brahma.

Revealing this above experience, he related an incident in his autobiography *Jeevan Smriti* as follows:

> I was 18 or 19 years old at that time. One early morning,
> I was standing in the veranda (porch) and saw the sunrise
> between the tree leaves. Suddenly, for a moment, I
> felt as if a curtain was removed from my eyes. I saw a
> world resplendent with wonderful glory. Happiness and

beauty were rippling everywhere. The depressive coatings in the various layers of my heart were instantly pierced and a universal radiance splashed inside me. I felt I was witnessing the truth through my liberated vision.

This 'Truth' which is Rabindranath's connection with the universe, has been his 'life's God' (*Jeevan Devata*) and a reflection of the nectar of happiness. This realisation of 'Brahma' illuminated the seer poet throughout his life.

This self-realisation manifested itself in the creation of his vast literary output, including thousands of songs, numerous drawings, and hundreds of letters. He earned recognition as a world poet and as a spokesperson of India's spiritual contribution to the world.

This spiritual foundation of Rabindranath embraced India's saints with open arms from his childhood onwards.

The names of some of these saints are worth mentioning here: Sri Ramkrishna Paramahansadev, *Mahayogi* Baherababa, Swami Vivekananda, Brahmabandhav Upadhaya, *Mahatma* Lalon Fakir, *Maramiya* Sadhak Gagan Bhattacharya, Ramananda Bharati, Bhupendranath Sanyal, *Mahatma* Krishnaramji, Dharmananda Bharati, *Mahatma* Bijoykrishna Goswami, *Parampurush* Sri Sri Bamakhyapa, Sister Nivedita, *Yogiraj* Ramnath Aghoribaba, *Rishi* Arabinda, *Khyapa Baul* Nabani Das, *Kriyayogi* Buddha Bose, and *Mahasadhika* Sri Sri Rangama.

All these saints had achieved enlightenment by following different religious paths derived from traditions such as Shakta, Shaiva, Ganpatya, Shoura, Brahma, and Aul Baul etc.

The four spiritual pillars of Indian sadhana namely knowledge, devotion, service, and yoga had led these saints to meet the supreme spirit.

Having been in the company of these enlightened individuals, Rabindranath had an immersive experience of Hindu spirituality. This illuminated soul truly reflected the embodiment of India's ancient sages. Therefore, this omniscient poet addressed his 'life's God' as follows:

Let all my flow of emotions,
Get rejuvenated in you today.

RAMKRISHNA

THE GREATEST spiritual sage and an incarnation of God of our age, Sri Ramkrishna, in his quest for association with spiritually enlightened persons, came to the residence of Maharshi Debendranath Tagore at Jorasanko, in 1868 to meet and share sacred thoughts with this household worshipper (*grihi sadhak*) and pursuer of the self-existing spirit (*Brahmabid*). He was accompanied by religious follower and attendant Sri Mathuranath Biswas aka 'Sejobabu'.

Sri Ramkrishna, who believed in the unity of all religions, had a unique and balanced perspective on who is defined as a saint (*sadhu*) and the necessity of spending time with saints.

In reply to a question from a devotee 'Who do you consider a *sadhu*?' Ramkrishna cheerfully answered, 'Anyone whose mind, life and inner soul are immersed in God, is a *sadhu*. That person, who has relinquished all worldly attachment, is a *sadhu*.'

When asked, 'What are the signs of a *sadhu*?', the saint from Dakshineshwar replied, 'A *sadhu*'s thoughts are always with God. He talks about God only. Realising that God is everywhere, he is always at the service of all created beings. He does not accumulate anything. This is the reason why the company of saints (*sadhu sangha*) is essential.'

RAMKRISHNA PARAMAHAMSA

'The seeking for God is the medicine to get rid of the disease of intense family attachment. To be in touch with God, one has to be in the company of saints. The family attachment and liberation, both are at the command of God. When he feels the time for liberation has come, he will arrange for the company of sadhus.'

Looking at the devotees he continued by saying, 'The hearts of saints are larger than those of others. That is why their company is required. Even saints require the company of saints.' He said this a trifle uneasily. because, he believed that constant association with householders addicted to worldly desires taints even the mind of saints. The company of other saints cleans, purifies the mind, and restores the sacred radiance. This is why even saints desire the company of other saints (*satsangha*).

Therefore, this realisation born out of direct experience by Ramkrishna, the incarnation of God, best among the saints, is extreme. His lively statements are in fact akin to the Biblical gospels. They are the word of God. It is in pursuance of this that Ramkrishna came to the residence of Maharshi Debendranath. To seek *satsangha*.

Mathur babu introduced this God incarnate to one-time classmate and friend Debendranath, 'This is Sri Ramkrishna Paramahansa. He has come to see you. He is insanely in love with God.'

Ramkrishna was pleased to see Maharshi Debendranath. He started the conversation in an easy and simple way.

With a calm and smiling face, this householder Brahmo *sadhak* and the founder of the Adi Brahmo Samaj, started talking with Ramkrishna. He also answered calmly the questions that were put to him by Ramkrishna.

Those who seek God, and do meditation, develop some divine marks in their bodies. In order to see those signs, Ramkrishna asked Debendranath 'Let me see your bare chest'. With a smile, Debendranath opened his shirt and bared his chest. Ramkrishna was delighted to note the reddish hue, like the colour of *sindur* (the vermilion mark worn in the parting by married Hindu women), that covered his otherwise fair-skinned chest.

According to tradition, those who seek God with all their heart and soul, meditate intensely, develop a reddish tinge from throat to navel.

Sri Ramkrishna was delighted to notice this validation of the scriptures. He also found out that Maharshi Debendranath was a yogi and a family man too. He saw that many children of Debendranath came to see him. Who can say that 7-year-old Rabindranath wasn't among those children? May be Rabindranath was there, curious to see Ramkrishna. It is possible that after meeting Ramkrishnadeb. his desire to meet divine personalities grew stronger.

Ramkrishna told the *Maharshi,* 'You are *Kaliyug's* leader.'

Humorously Ramkrishna said, 'The leader looks at both sides to ensure nobody is watching and then drinks the milk from the pot.' This line was borrowed from a parody written by Aju Goshai (Ayodhya Nath Goswami), itself based on the words of the mystic Ramprasad, Goshai's neighbor, who had said, 'This world is the home of deceptions.'

Ramkrishna said to Maharshi Debendranath, 'I have come to see you because I heard that despite being a householder, you have kept your mind focused on God. Let me hear some spiritual words from you.' In response, Maharshi quoted some words from the Vedas. He said, 'This world is like a chandelier and its inhabitants are like individual lamps nestled inside the chandelier. God has created humans through whom He illuminates His glory. If the lamps don't light up, the chandelier remains dark. You don't even notice the chandelier.'

Ramkrishna enjoyed this statement. He had made a similar philosophical statement sitting beneath the Panchavati tree in Dakshineswar. Maharshideb cordially invited Ramkrishna to join their Brahmo festivities.

Later on 2 May 1883, a Wednesday, the youngest son of Maharshi Debendranath, Rabindranath at the age of 22 came to Kashi Mitra's villa in the suburbs, to attend Brahmo Samaj celebrations and sang the song written by him in front of the chief guest Sri Ramkrishnadev. His song went as follows:

I have made you the polestar of my life.

Ne'er again shall I be lost in this ocean.

Wherever I roam, may your presence be felt,

Pour down your sunbeam on my earnest teardrops.

Always in my mind your face appears secretly,

Even a moment of disappearance makes me see no shore,

no land.

If on any occasion, this heart is confused and goes the

wrong way -

Instantly seeing your face makes me embarrassed.

While listening to this song, Ramkrishna gradually went into deep contemplation and Rabindranath watched this transformation of Ramakrishna in quiet wonder.

Watching this change in the divine son of Mother Kali, Rabindranath might have remembered that just two years ago (1881), at the age of twenty, while creating the music for the dance drama *Balmiki Pratibha*, he had composed two songs dedicated to Mother Kali. Though he was brought up in the environment of the Brahmo Samaj, he had written these two songs for the Hindu Goddess Kali. The transliteration is as follows:

Kaali *kaali* balo re aaj -
Balo ho, ho ho, balo ho, ho ho, balo ho.
Naamer jore saadhibo kaaj -
Balo ho ho ho, balo ho, balo ho.
Oi ghor matto kare nrityo rango-maajhare,
Oi lokkho lokkho jokkho rokkho gheri shyamare,
Oi latto-patto-kesh, atto atto haase re -
Haha hahaha hahaha.
Aare bal re shyama maayer joy, joy joy.
Joy joy, joy joy, joy joy, joy joy,
Aare bal re shyama mayer joy, joy joy,
Aare bal re shyama maayer joy.

(Heartfelt offering and reverence to Mother Kali)

For the first song *Kali Kali balo re aaj*, Rabindranath borrowed the music from one of the famous English ballads. However, on 2 May 1883, Ramkrishna enjoyed the Brahmo

Samaj celebrations at the Nandan garden, in particular, the song (*tomarei koriachi jiboner dhrubotara*), written and composed by Rabindranath which had touched his heart.

Ramkrishna joyfully praised the song. There was another occasion on which Ramkrishna had gone into a trance after listening to Rabindra sangeet. That song was sung by his principal disciple Narendranath Dutta (later Swami Vivekananda) in his own room at Dakshineswar. It will be discussed later at the appropriate place. Observing Sri Ramkrishna who was invited as the chief guest at the Brahmo Samaj celebration, it is difficult to gauge whether Rabindranath's childhood memory of Sri Ramkrishna's visit to his ancestral home, came back to him.

Later, in the last years of his life, Tagore presided over the assembly of religions constituted on the occasion of Ramkrishna's birth centenary celebration at the Calcutta University Institute Hall on 3 March 1936. At the age of 75, he paid respect to Ramkrishna in presence of famous dignitaries from India and abroad, by giving a perfect lecture which was acknowledged by one and all. He showered praise on Ramkrishna 'for proving his own sacred spiritual realisation in a barren age full of religious anarchy'.

'The largeness of his spirit could comprehend seemingly antagonistic modes of *sadhana*, and the simplicity of his soul shames for all time the pomp and pedantry of pontiffs and pundits. Enlightened souls like Ramkrishna have realised the truth in its totality. They have the power to feel the oneness in everything and realise the overall justification of the different manifestations of the truth.'

In addition to this tribute, Tagore also expressed his deep reverence for Sri Ramkrishna Paramahansadev through this poem:

> Diverse *courses* of worship
> from varied springs of fulfillment
> have mingled in your meditation.
> The manifold revelation of the joy of the Infinite
> has given form to a shrine of unity in your life,
> where from far and near arrive salutations
> to which I join my own.

Not only that, but he also appreciated the various charitable activities of the Ramkrishna Mission with great reverence. He sent good wishes to Ramkrishna Medical Education Society by saying, 'All the selfless charitable works that are being carried out silently are a testament to the great reverence and respect in which his memories are held.'

During his life, Rabindranath came across many saints, but he experienced greater exaltation in the company of Sri Ramkrishna and his disciples.

He had the opportunity of having the divine company of Ramkrishna, Swami Vivekananda, Sister Nivedita, Swami Abhedananda, and other members of the Ramkrishna Mission. He met them more than once. However, the influence of Sri Ramkrishna, Swami Vivekananda and Sister Nivedita was unforgettable. It will be discussed more in detail later.

BAHERA BABA

MORE THAN one year after the Brahmo Samaj celebration at Nandan Bagan, North Calcutta, Rabindranath got married on 9 December 1884. Maharshi Debendranath Tagore brought the famous ancient Mahayogi Bahera Baba of Gyanganj in the Himalayas, to this wedding at his Jorasanko residence. It was his earnest desire to see his youngest son Rabindranath and the new bride Mrinalini Devi being blessed by this holy man. The Maharshi had met this great and enlightened saint on one of his trips to the Himalayas when the latter had descended from the hills of Gyanganj to the foothills.

The epicenter of India's spiritual activity is Gyanmath aka Gyanganj. It is located in a remote area north of the Manasarovar in the snow-clad Himalayan mountains. Though it is visible, only yogis who have achieved transcendental status, can enter this place. However, if a yogi or an ardent spiritual seeker receives grace from a saint of the highest order, he or she can enter this site when accompanied by that saint. The transcendental centre is situated at a much higher elevation than Gyanganj. Only in the form of a subtle (fine) body can one enter that arena. The main creation center of the universe is stationed in this divine abode from time immemorial.

At this great experimental center, saints (both men and women) who have reached the peak of their *sadhana*, have been

GYANGANJ

working tirelessly, secretly, and silently in the scientific pursuit of knowledge in various subjects namely air, sky, stars, moon, ocean, land surface and others. The ages of these transcendental yogis vary between 200 to 2000 years. In this divine place, there is no disease, old age, and death—only perpetual spring.

This Gyanganj controls India's spiritual power and its advancement. Not only that, this heavenly abode also controls and maintains spiritual thoughts, power, and advancement for the whole world.

Being more than 100 years old, Bahera Baba was an expert in wind science and earth science. Adopting wind science, he could control the five elements of the body, and would transform and travel in his astral body thousands of miles within seconds and materialise into his human body at will to be with his disciples. Sometimes on his own free will, Bahera Baba, for the benefit of his disciples, would present himself in physical body at different places at the same time.

Since Bahera Baba was proficient in earth science also, he could predict who would be visiting him that day by touching the earth.

Sri Sri Bishudhananda Paramahansa was another Mahayogi from Gyanganj. His disciple was the world-famous philosopher Mahamahopadhyaya Doctor Gopinath Kaviraj. In Kashi, Bishudhananda was also well known as *Gandha baba* (perfume saint). He became an expert in solar science from Gyanganj. With his yogic power, he could create any substance from sunlight. He also created life in front of several learned and knowledgeable people. In his ashram at Kashi, people were mystified by these miracles. He also cured many incurable diseases with his yogic power. In fact, Gyanganj's solar science is a completely tested spiritual science. Inherent life power of the inert as well as conscious matter of the world exists in a latent state within the sunlight. That is why the sun is the source of life for this world and its inhabitants. So, all the objects in the world have life embedded within and that life is everywhere.

Swami Bishudhananda, therefore, could create precious stones from simple cotton with the help of sunlight. From a scrap of paper, he created a butterfly that flew inside the room before escaping out into the sky. Whatever he wanted, he could create instantly from the rays of the sun. India's famous saint Ma Anandamoyee, on her visit to Kashi, observed this strange phenomenon of solar science. Later, the famous philosopher, Surendranath Dasgupta was impressed by observing the creation of a butterfly from a piece of paper with the help of solar science. Seeing the creation, from an inert substance to a living butterfly escaping out into the sky, mesmerised Dasgupta. He discussed this miraculous act with Rabindranath in later years with due reverence.

Bishudhananda Paramahansa subsequently brought a very old *Shivalinga*—dating from the era of the Mahabharata—from Gyanganj and installed it in his village Bandul near Burdwan. He named this all ambitious and accomplished Shivalinga, Bandeleswar.

The spiritual and mystic bond between Gyanganj and this holy Shivalinga has existed for the last half a century. All enlightened yogis visualise this at that location just before dawn (the exact moment when body and mind are in unison).

Another famous mahayogi, with miraculous power, Sri Sri Ramthakur was also from Gyanganj. His many unbelievable acts received attention across India.

Maharshideb while staying with Bahera Baba in the Himalayas, learnt *Kriya* yoga and became an expert in earth science.

Once some people from Calcutta came to visit Maharshideb at the Santiniketan *brahmachari* ashram. They arrived in the afternoon and were surprised to find the food already cooked and ready for them. The same day in the morning, Maharshideb had informed the cook that four visitors from Calcutta were coming to the Ashram and food should be prepared for them. They had come without informing Maharshideb. On enquiry, Maharshideb explained that in the morning he had touched the earth and had perceived four people coming to visit him from Calcutta.

Sometime later, Maharshideb invited Mahayogi Bahera Baba to his Ashram at Santiniketan. After that, he took him to Jorasanko. This is where several people had his *darshan* and many of them received his blessings. Along with his brothers, the 21-year-old poet and songwriter Rabindranath had the darshan of Bahera Baba.

During this time (1882), Rabindranath composed a beautiful song dedicated to his mother. He had lost his mother at a very young age and naturally craved his mother's affection. This he had expressed through countless songs over the course of his life. He expressed his feelings as a child deprived of a mother's love, by writing songs dedicated to the motherly universe and motherland.

We reproduce here an *example* of such a song written and composed at the age of 21.

> With the high hope I have come, let me come closer,
>
> Force me not outside, Holy Mother.
>
> Acceptance is lower for the poor and the downtrodden
>
> You'll accept me - I am sure.
>
> My requisites are simple, allow me to stay at your feet.
>
> My requisites are simple, allow me to call you 'My Mother'.
>
> Unless you accept me where do I find a home,
>
> Where would I roam about crying -
>
> There I can see the dark, veiled, terrifying night.

However, Mahayogi Bahera Baba, after a few days, left for the Himalayas from the Jorasanko residence. The following year, upon invitation from Maharshideb, Bahera Baba came back to Calcutta.

On an earnest request from Maharshideb, Bahera Baba reached the Maharshi's youngest son Rabindranath's marriage ceremony venue on 9 December 1888. After the marriage, the newlywed couple, Rabindranath and Mrinalini Devi, upon instruction from Maharshideb, prostrated themselves at Bahera Baba's feet to show obeisance. Maharshideb requested Bahera Baba to bless this couple.

Mahayogi Bahera Baba looked at the couple and their future became apparent to this seer's eyes. He blessed the couple and then calmly said to the Maharshi 'This youngest son of yours will be world famous. He will perceive the divine and achieve Brahma consciousness. But his wife's longevity will be short. Her family life will also not be happy.'

Later on in life, this seer's prediction came true. Rabindranath received the Nobel Prize and became world famous. He did achieve divine realisation and Brahma consciousness which manifested itself in his composed songs and literature. This was also reflected in his art, numerous letters, lectures, and short articles. In real life, his wife died untimely at a very young age. As a result, Rabindranath had to go through a lot of anxiety and unhappiness because of his children (Madhurilata, Rathindranath, Renuka, Meera and Shamindranath).

Especially, the untimely death of his two daughters, Madhuri and Renuka, and his youngest son Shamindranath caused him immense pain and grief. He bore this pain till his death. Moreover, he never got peace with his surviving son, Rathindranath and daughter Meera. He expressed this pain and hurt in several letters.

Thus, he never achieved happiness in his family life. Bahera Baba's predictions came true. Rabindranath was always respectful to him. Bahera Baba was born in a famous Tewari family at Chapra, Bihar. In his youth, with the help of a realised soul, he reached Gyanganj and after a long sadhana, he became expert in the sciences of air and earth.

His Guru named him Bahera Baba. Later on, he came down to the plains guided by his preordained spiritual responsibility and established an Ashram in Beniapur, near Chapra district.

He was a worshipper of Durga Devi. The news of his miraculous powers slowly spread across India. In 1883, when Rabindranath and his wife met Bahera Baba at their wedding reception, his age was about 100 years.

He went on to live for another 100 years at his own wish and remained healthy and free from disease. India's spiritual leaders, intellectuals, and persons from all walks of life, benefited from his blessings.

In West Bengal, more than one chief minister, education minister, party leaders, literary figures, businesspersons (Jugal Kishore Birla, R N Goenka, P N Pansai) government and non-government employees, and numerous other individuals were fortunate enough to receive divine blessings from Bahera Baba.

On 2 December 1979, he willfully took on himself an incurable disease from his disciple to save him and left his mortal body at the age of 200 years in Calcutta (Bellevue Nursing Home).

VIVEKANANDA

ON THE pleasant evening of 14 September 1884, a 21-year-old good looking young man Narendra Dutta (later known as Swami Vivekananda), was singing a song in his melodious voice to Sri Ramkrishna in Ramakrishna's room in Dakshineswar. The song, written by 23-year-old Rabindranath was as follows:

> After day and night's careful efforts
>
> I have created a place in my heart -
>
> Oh Lord, would you be kind enough to come here.
>
> This place is very peaceful and calm,
>
> I have carefully created this place in the privacy of my clean heart.
>
> Outside lamp, sun and moon will not provide the flow of light,
>
> Only you, God, can provide the effulgence over there.
>
> Far away from the desires, flirtations, noise, and entertainment
>
> Sentiments of owning wealth have fled far away.
>
> Only happiness reigns there in total silence –
>
> Will be your priest, Lord, in your service only –
>
> Sitting in silence continually, shedding teardrops at your feet,
>
> Will remain awake at the door alone closing tearful eyes.

Swami Vivekananda

Narendranath was deeply absorbed in singing this song. People present in the room were listening with rapt attention. While listening to the song, Sri Ramkrishna went into deep contemplation and after some time he stepped down from his cot and sat down next to Narendranath who was immersed in rendering the song.

Earlier, on 2 May 1883, at Kashi Mitra's Nandan Garden, during the Brahmo Samaj Festival, 22 years old Rabindranath Tagore sang the song written by him, 'I have made you the guiding star', in front of Sri Ramkrishna which sent him into a trance. On 14 September 1888, with great happiness and feeling, he was hearing a song composed by the same Rabindranath, sung by his would-be disciple and follower, Narendranath. Both these scenarios were incredible. In one scenario, the singer was Rabindranath and in the other it was Narendranath. The common listener was the incarnation of God, Sri Ramkrishna.

Since Ramkrishna was himself a great singer and lover of music, he became absorbed listening to the melodious songs from both Rabindranath and Narendra Nath. Invisibly Ramkrishna's generous blessings were being showered on both these singers. Later in life, both of them got astonishing recognition on the world stage in different disciplines by different paths. One became a world poet and the other became world famous by teaching Hindu spirituality to the rest of the world. Two great human beings became the spokespersons for the soul of India.

The difference in age between Rabindranath and

Vivekananda was merely one year eight months and five days. Vivekananda was born on 12 January 1863 and Rabindranath was born on 7 May 1861. Though Rabindranath was the elder of the two, their acquaintance, intrinsic connection, and good will were deeply rooted.

Vivekananda, who was then inspired by Brahmo philosophy, sang another song of Rabindranath, at the wedding reception (on 29 July 1881) of Krishna Kumar Mitra (editor of *Sanjivani Patrika* and leader of the independence movement) at the Brahmo Samaj Mandir. The song composed by Rabindranath was as follows:

If the rivers of two hearts meet
Tell me where it runs in full earnest.
Your ocean of love is in front of them,
They both want to mingle in your boundless heart.
They met together with same aspiration,
They are walking towards the same goal.
Hundreds of obstacles are on the way, full of rocky mountain,
Combined strength will break through that.
Finally, when the great journey of life ends,
May you then give shelter in your arms of love.
Happiness of two hearts, sorrows of two hearts
The aspirations of two hearts will finally rest at your feet.

Prior to singing this song, Rabindranath taught the younger Narendranath how to sing this song. Narendranath sang this song in his beautiful voice, and impressed everybody present there. Narendranath's age was only 18 years, six months, and seventeen days at that time. There were four songs of Rabindranath presented on this occasion (29 July 1881). Just like he taught Narendranath to sing *Dui hridoyer nadi akotra mililo jodi* (if the rivers of two hearts meet), he taught three other songs *Jagater purohit tumi* (You are the priest of the world), *Shubhodine eseche dhonhe*, (On this auspicious day, you two have come) *Mahaguru duti chatro eseche tomar* (Great master, two students have come to you) to singers Nagendranath Chattopadhyay, Sundar Mohan Das and the blind Chunilal. These songs were sung by these artists in front of the wedding guests that day. Krishna Kumar Mitra got married to Rishi Rajnarayan Basu's fourth daughter Lilavati. It was apparent that Rabindranath knew the guests well—both from the groom's and the bride's side. He must have known the four singers, too, otherwise he wouldn't have taught his own compositions to them.

In this way, young Narendranath sang young Rabindranath's composed songs at different congregations with love and respect. However, before discussing his closeness to Rabindranath, other facts need to be emphasised. Apart from singing his songs on several occasions, Narendranath also wrote notations for Rabindranath's songs with great sincerity. When Narendranath's age was around 23 years (1885-1886), he was going through the most adverse situations in his life. Despite this and prior to leaving his family permanently, he wrote this wonderful book *Sangeet Pada Kalpataru* (The Wish-yielding Musical Verses). In addition to his own compositions and other famous song writers' songs, he also did the notations of Rabindranath's songs, in the volume.

Many people are not aware that outside the confines of the Jorasanko Tagore residence, an outsider Narendranath (later Swami Vivekananda), for the first time, had written notations for Rabindra Sangeet. During this time, Rabindranath who was hardly 25 years old, was only known within the circle of the acolytes of the Brahmo Samaj. Narendranath was not even 23 years old when he sang Rabindra sangeet and gave notations to the songs.

Narendranath knew by heart the devotional songs written by many famous writers. Despite this, he took the time to write the notations of the lesser-known Rabindranath's songs very diligently.

The book *Sangeet pada Kalpataru* is a testament to the great musical knowledge and talent of Narendranath. Written during a tumultuous period of his life, the book reveals his extraordinary talent, personality, hard work, focus and concentration. The book has two parts. The first part reflects the depth of Narendranath's knowledge of Indian music. The second part includes his writings on Shyama Sangeet (songs dedicated to the goddess Kali), Sri Krishna Vaishnav songs, Christian and Islamic religious songs.

Narendranath had visited Jorasanko Tagore residence several times. Rabindranath's elder brother Dwijendranath Tagore's elder son Dwipendranath was a classmate of Narendranath. Both of them used to study at the same college. Rabindranath was only one year older than his nephew. That is why the relationship between uncle and nephew was deep and being peers, they had sincere discussions on several topics which included literature, culture, and music.

In the meantime, Narendranath visited the congregations of the Brahmo Samaj and gradually came close to Rabindranath. Therefore, he sang Rabindranath's songs at different musical gatherings.

Whenever Narendranath came to visit his classmate, Dwipendranath used to invite his favourite Rabi uncle to his room, and they used to have a great get together. The meetings would involve discussions on music or sometimes literature. Narendranath was an active participant in this group. In his deep and melodious voice, he used to sing a variety of songs to the accompaniment of a tanpura. The songs would include dhrupad, Brahmo sangeet, geet or bhajans. Rabindranath and Dwipendranath used to listen to these songs with rapt attention and admiration. Sometimes upon being requested by Narendranath and Dwipendranath, Rabindranath also used to sing. He generally sang his own compositions. They also had discussions on Brahmo Dharma and the Brahmo Samaj.

While participating in these discussions, Narendra used to boldly convey his own opinions, which Rabindranath accepted respectfully. Sometimes at the request of Dwipendranath, he used to sing Tagore songs which Rabindranath used to listen to with humility and appreciation. In this way, Rabindranath had come into close contact with Narendranath, over a long period of time. In future, whatever Rabindranath spoke in praise of Narendranath (Swami Vivekananda), was a result of this close relationship.

Rabindranath's own nature was very courteous and gentle. Narendranath also used to love and respect this handsome, soft spoken, talented person. Both Narendranath and Rabindranath had the broadness of mind to give proper dignity to qualified persons. Therefore, from the very first meeting, both had mutual respect for each other.

The age differences between the three individuals were interesting. Rabindranath (1861), Dwipendranath (1862) and Narendranath (1863) were like three marked fruits of the Kalpa tree, rich in nectar. Dwipendranath especially played a very important role as a facilitator creating a bridge between these two future world-famous personalities.

That is why the worlds of literature, culture and spiritual exertion have remained ever grateful to Dwipendranath Tagore, who himself remaining silent, unseen and almost anonymous acting as a bridge between these two future world leaders.

Another person who was also instrumental in creating this bridge was Hemlata Tagore, the wife of Dwipendranath. Hemlata Tagore was also very close to Rabindranath, who taught her English and Sanskrit.

Hemlata Tagore (1873-1967) was the great-great granddaughter Raja Ram Mohan Roy's granddaughter, a reformer and modern thinker. Therefore, she was considered a bridge between Ram Mohan and Rabindranath.

Even after completion of their student life, Dwipendranath and Narendranath remained strongly connected throughout their lives. Though Narendranath often attended Brahmo Samaj congregations, his deep yearning to experience the divinity in its other forms (duality) arose. One day he came across Maharshi Debendranath Tagore (Rabindranath's father) at Jorasanko and with his large, wide-open eyes, directly asked Maharshi, 'Sir, have you seen God?' The Maharshi gave him a bewitched look. Then he told him about the realisation of Brahma. The Maharshi was probably not aware that Narendranath was his eldest grandson's classmate since the Maharshi didn't know the identity of so many people that visited his residence daily. However, looking at this young man, in a happy tone he said, 'You have beautiful eyes.'

This did not satisfy the spiritually inquisitive mind of Narendranath. After some time, he had the opportunity to visit Sri Ramkrishna at Dakshineswar. This is where he got the answers to all his questions, which are well known to all of us.

Though he left Brahmo Samaj and slowly came under the spiritual umbrella of Sri Ramkrishna, Narendranath's ties with the Tagore family were never broken. Upon cordial invitations from the newly wed close friend Dwipendranath and his loving wife Hemlata Tagore, Narendra used to visit their Jorasanko residence. Maharshideb was very affectionately attached to his eldest granddaughter-in-law. She used to lovingly feed her elderly grandfather-in-law daily rice pudding with her own hands from a golden bowl with a gold spoon.

Hemlata Tagore was a poet by nature. Later in life, numerous poems by her were published in different journals and newspapers. Rabindranath, her uncle-in-law, himself was interested in her poetry and he took the initiative to publish them. Through his efforts, subsequently, her work was published in a book *Alor Pakhi* (Radiant Bird), edited by Kalidas Nag in 1935.

In later years, in the Tagore household and in Santiniketan, she was well known as Baroma (Elder Mother). Even Rabindranath's contemporary admirers, Prime Minister Jawaharlal Nehru, and West Bengal's Chief Minister Dr Bidhan Chandra Roy, respectfully called her *Baroma*.

It is known from the life history of Hemlata Tagore (1873-1967), that when she arrived as a 16 year-old newlywed wife to her husband's residence (1889), then Dwipendranath's age was 27. And his uncle Rabindranath's age was 28. For a long period of 52 years, Hemlata Tagore had the opportunity to observe the poet closely in a family setting. No other Tagore family wives had this unique good opportunity.

At the time Hemlata Tagore arrived at her husband's residence, Dwipendranath's dear friend Narendranath was 26 years old. From time to time, she used to invite Narendranath to their residence. Narendranath used to start singing with the help of a tanpura. Singing was Narendranath's passion. With deep concentration, he used to keep on singing one song after another. Dwipendranath and Hemlata listened to the songs, mesmerised, and with tearful eyes. Sometimes, Rabindranath used to join the group after being informed about Narendranath's visit. With deep appreciation, he also listened to those songs. Some days, at the request of Dwipendranath, Narendranath ate with them. Hemlata devi came to know from her husband what food Narendranath liked and she not only cooked the food but also served the food with her own hands. Hemlata had a good reputation for her cooking ability. Both Rabindranath and Narendranath praised her cooking while sitting and eating next to each other.

Not only were Dwipendranath and Hemlata fascinated by Narendranath's diverse talents and uplifting spirit, Rabindranath himself was impressed. Despite adverse situations in his personal life, Narendranath used to keep Dwipendranath and his wife Hemlata devi amused with his humor. His Guru Sri Ramakrishna, whom he loved more than his life, had passed away from earthly life. Most of his fellow disciples had dispersed in different directions in order to complete their disciplined spiritual practice or *sadhana*. Some remained in Alambazar Math, and some left for places like Haridwar. In the meantime, Narendra had already visited different places in northern India on foot and was preparing to go to other places in pursuit of his spiritual quest which involved the practice of austerities. He had almost cut his family ties. Despite being in the midst of this catastrophe, he kept on happily singing with an easy smile and maintaining a pleasant demeanor.

Rabindranath, Dwipendranath and Hemlata devi had observed Narendranath's deep spiritual thirst for a long time and were very impressed. Their belief that Narendra was an 'authoritative person' was deeply embedded within them. In later life, Narendra as Swami Vivekananda, came back to his country as a world-renowned person. However, his link with the Tagore family never snapped. A single comment by Rabindranath was a testament to his deep respect and admiration for Swami Vivekananda. In later years, he respectfully made the statement 'If you want to know India, you need to understand Vivekananda.' This deeply respectful attitude of Rabindranath contained a great deal of truth.

In the early mid nineteenth century, the modern reformer of subjugated India, Raja Ram Mohan Roy, was the first person to establish India's glory in England and Europe in the period 1830-1833.

Thereafter, in the late nineteenth century (7 August 1893 to be precise), Swami Vivekananda through his electrifying speech, raised the flag of glory for Hinduism at the Parliament of Religions in Chicago in the United States of America.

The representative of the world's most ancient religion, advocate of the Vedanta, the wise and bold Swami was only 30 years old at that time. He became world famous at that young age. Swami Vivekananda, the representative, and spokesperson for the soul of India, returned home after conquering America and Europe with his dynamic message of a resurgent Hindu faith in 1897. Swamiji was then 34 years old, and Rabindranath's age was 36 years. Fifteen years later, Rabindranath became world famous when he received the Nobel Prize. When Swami Vivekananda returned to India, a big reception for him was organised in Calcutta, by the fellow disciples of Sri Ramkrishna. The organisers, however, did not remember to invite the less known poet Rabindranath Tagore.

It was not unusual for his guru brothers not to remember to invite Rabindranath, since he was relatively unknown at that time.

The organisers, however, didn't forget to invite Rabindranath as the chief guest at the Parliament of Religions, on the occasion of Sri Ramkrishna's birth centenary in 1936. At this gathering, he showed his respect by giving his memorable tribute to Ramkrishna. Rabindranath would have given the same respectful tribute to Swamiji had he been invited to Swamiji's reception in 1897. In later times, on several occasions Rabindranath did offer his appreciation for Swamiji's achievements.

From the memoirs of Hemlata Tagore (Baroma), it was apparent that after hearing of the reception of Swami Vivekananda in 1897, the entire Tagore family was excited and happy. Maharshi Debendranath and Rabindranath had sincerely wanted to give a reception and congratulate Swami Vivekananda for his achievement at the Jorasanko residence, where people from all walks of life, irrespective of caste, creed and colour would be able to attend.

However, due to the vehement opposition of the Brahmo leader Pratap Chandra Majumdar and some of his followers, they had to sacrifice their great desire to host the event. Pratap Chandra Majumdar from the very beginning of the meeting of Chicago Parliament of Religions, had shown opposition towards Swami Vivekananda, due to jealousy and he even tried to convince the organisers that Swamiji was not a representative of the Hindu religion. However, when Swamiji ignoring all opposition, earned unparalleled fame and respect, from the world at large, Pratap Chandra, fueled by mere jealousy, started to attack Swamiji's character viciously after the latter returned to India. Because of this unreasonable opposition from Pratap Chandra Majumdar, Maharshideb and Rabindranath, couldn't invite Swami Vivekananda to their residence. Brahmo Samaj had already been divided into three fractions – Adi Brahmo Samaj, Ordinary Brahmo Samaj and the New Brahmo Samaj. They did not want another division on account of this reception. However, Rabindranath was always unique in his own right. He expressed his unbounded respect and love for Swami Vivekananda several times to his countrymen in future years. He said, 'Vivekananda's message was that – Brahma's power was embedded within every human being – and through the poor, Narayan (God) demands our service (seva). His unique message showed a new path for humanity treading on which it would be possible to achieve self-realisation and salvation by transcending selfishness.' This powerful message of achieving salvation through selfless service to humanity and following the path of renunciation, encouraged our youth.

In relation to Vivekananda, Rabindranath wrote to the famous western philosopher and writer Romain Rolland, 'In him everything is positive and nothing negative.' He also wrote, 'If you want to know India, then learn about Vivekananda.'

He wrote with deep respect, 'These messages of Vivekananda are calls to the human soul'. This is how Rabindranath expressed his reverence for Vivekananda time and again. A surprising matching of souls between these two greats has been noticed. In the material world, Swami Vivekananda met and associated with three generations of the Tagore family namely, Maharshi Debendranath, Rabindranath and Dwipendranath. In the spiritual plane, Rabindranath met and also associated with Sri Ramkrishna, Swami Vivekananda, and sister Nivedita.

> The older I grow, the more everything seems to me to lie in manliness. This is my new gospel.
>
> —Swami Vivekanada

Two great spokespersons of Mother India's soul, though divergent in their paths, were united in their minds and they radiated mutual love and respect towards each other.

BRAHMABANDHAB

WITHIN BRAHMABANDHAB there existed a unique combination of Hinduism, Brahmo dharma, and Christianity. He was well known as a Vedantic, celibate, truthful, fearless, patriotic and a great revolutionary. Young Rabindranath had a deep respect for him. Rabindranath used to pay careful attention to the spiritual discussions Brahmabandhab used to have with Maharshi Debendranath. Slowly Rabindranath got deeply attracted towards Brahmabandhab Upadhyay.

In 1887, when Rabindranath was 26 years old, this ardent Hindu ascetic and Vedantic, Brahmabandhab Upadhyay got deeply attracted towards unconditioned, eternal, formless Brahma, and joined the Brahmo dharma or faith. He was initiated into the Brahmo religion at the Nababidhan Brahmo Samaj established by Keshab Chandra Sen. During this time, Rabindranath came in close contact with him and was very impressed by him.

Brahmabandhab was not only a great Vedantic but was equally great as a revolutionary. This strange character who combined highly opposing forces deeply moved Rabindranath. Fortified by his own beliefs, Brahmabandhab used to go forward, often alone, to achieve his goal. Rabindranath observed it closely. Rabindranath wrote a song at this time (1890) as follows:

BRAHMABANDHAB UPADHYAY

I am walking *alone* in this world,
Who will help me find my way?
Fear not, fear not –
Travel at your free will
Just like bees flocking
Only towards the fragrance of flowers.

This song perfectly depicts the character traits (Vedantic as well as revolutionary) of Brahmabandhab Upadhyay.

Gradually Brahmabandhab Upadhyay jumped into the freedom movement and very soon became well known in the ranks of the revolutionaries.

In 1891, Brahmabandhab Upadhyay suddenly left the Brahmo Samaj, went to Hyderabad and became a Christian. Despite this, Rabindranath and the nation's Hindu and Brahmo leaders did not lose their faith in and respect for him.

Whatever his personal beliefs might have been, his great talent and the love for his country were even bigger. Hence, his leaving the Brahmo Samaj and becoming a Christian, did not diminish Rabindranath's deep respect for him. Rabindranath respectfully said, 'On the one hand he is a Roman Catholic Sannyasi; on the other, he is Vedantic, courageous and fearless, a selfless individual, a powerful speaker and a very influential person.'

After embracing Christianity and remaining a Christian for 15 years, in 1907 Brahmabandhab Upadhyay gave up Christianity and returned to the Hindu faith.

A few years later, he was arrested by the British administration, convicted for preaching revolution against the British in the newspaper *Sandhya* brought out by the *Anushilan Samiti*, a revolutionary organisation, and that he edited. 'During the trial, Brahmabandhab reported pain in the abdomen and was admitted to the Campbell hospital of Calcutta. He succumbed to death on 27 October 1907 at the age of 46'.

Rabindranath, who always recognised talent, remained ever respectful towards Brahmabandhab Upadhyay throughout his life.

LALON FAKIR

WHEN RABINDRANATH'S age was 27 years old (1888), he came to Shilaidaha, in East Bengal's Kustia district, to oversee his estate. This is the place where he met the enlightened mystic devotee Lalon Fakir on several occasions.

Lalon Fakir's life and sadhana were full of diversity. The 27 year-old Rabindranath was fascinated by this ancient mystic Baul singer. His famous Baul songs were highly spiritual and metaphorical. Among his many songs, one famous song fascinated Rabindranath deeply. It goes as follows:

> *How an unidentified bird*
> *Comes inside the cage and flies away.*
> *If I could catch the bird*
> *I would tie my mind's fetters to the bird's feet.*

Rabindranath used this song in his novel *Gora*. Lalon Fakir's generous nature and mystic devotion impressed Rabindranath deeply. An idealised 'inner being' (*moner manush)* derived from a Baul concept and uniting that with beautiful Baul compositions in harmony with nature attracted Rabindranath very much. Rabindranath could find a similarity between the message of the Upanishads and the inner meaning of Baul songs.

MAHATMA LALON FAKIR

The great message of the Upanishads, *Tang vedyang purushong veda ma bo mrityu parivyatha* (Know only the Supreme being to be known, otherwise it is only the pain of death). The Bauls remain absorbed in happiness having realised that this Supreme Being is none other than their own inner being.

The more Rabindranath came in contact with the mystic Lalon Fakir and listened to his spiritually enriched, precious Baul songs, the more he came under the influence of this music.

Having been bathed in Baul language and composition, Rabindranath introduced himself later as 'Rabindra Baul'. He stated, 'I have included their compositions in many of my songs. The Baul melody and message have merged within me unnoticed.'

Here is one of the simplest examples of how the melody and feeling of a Baul song had influenced Rabindranath:

Lalon Fakir wrote:

> *Sailor of my mind, control and stabilise the boat, which is*
> *about to sink,*
> *Family is withering under heavy storm.*

Rabindranath wrote (imitating the Baul tune)

> *Now that tide has splashed on to your perched river,*
> *Set sail your boat, chanting "victory for mother".*

Again, Lalon wrote:

> *In my mind's imagination I saw the inner being made of*
> *pure gold*
> *Sadly, when I try to catch it, it eludes me.*

Rabindranath wrote (imitating the Baul tune):
Oh, my friend, when will you steal my mind,
By breaking the shackles of myself.

Mahatma Lalon Fakir's disciple was *sadhak* (devotee) Fakir Chand. Rabindranath was delighted to hear about the eventful and ascetic life history of Lalon Fakir. Lalon was Hindu by birth but through his life's work became a Muslim. He was born in Bhobra village, which was part of Kumarkhali in Kustia District. He was born in 1774. His real name was Lalon Chandra Kar. His father's name was Madhab Chandra Kar. Once during his youth, Lalon travelled to Santipur in Nadia District to take a bath in the Ganges. All of a sudden, he had an attack of smallpox and became unconscious. Assuming he was dead, his relatives let his body float away in the river. At that time, a Muslim couple picked him up from the river and nursed him back to life.

In the meantime, Lalon's household got the news that Lalon had died. In time, his last rites were completed. After some time, when Lalon came back home, his relatives declined to accept him. Even his elderly mother and young wife did not agree to let him in the house in fear of societal compulsions. The main reason was his last rites had already been performed, his taking shelter in a Muslim family and accepting their food.

Deeply hurt and disappointed, Lalon left his home forever. He came to Cheuria a village near the Kustia Railway station. There he found shelter with a Muslim Baul Fakir by the name Sirajsai. He learned Baul songs and the playing of the instrument called sarangi. Gradually he became Sirajsai's disciple. Slowly, he became famous as Lalon Fakir. Sirajsai also became famous as Lalon's guru.

A great bridge maker between Hindus and Muslims—Lalon Fakir had well-wishers and admirers like Shivchandra Bidyanarbo and Kangal Harinath, famous tantriks (worshipper of Divine Mother) of Kumarkhali, Kustia.

One day, sitting in the residence of Shivchandra (Sarvo Mangala Temple), old Lalon Fakir, while playing his sarangi, composed some Baul songs extempore and shared with those present there. The song goes like this:

Everyone asks whether Lalon is Hindu or non-Hindu,

Lalon says he has no clue.

On the same shore people come and go

The same sailor is sailing the boat.

People don't eat food touched by others.

Where do people find different water?

Rabindranath first met Lalon Fakir in 1888 when old Lalon was 114 years old. One year later, on 5 May, Rabindranath requested his elder brother Jyotirindranath to draw a sketch of this 115-year-old great mystic saint, Lalon Fakir. The following year, on 17 October 1890, at the age of 116 years, Lalon Fakir passed away at his residence of *sadhana* at Cheuria village.

Rabindranath, who came in close contact with Lalon Fakir, and being an admirer of his talent, took 20 of Lalon's songs and published them for the first time in the *Probashi* newspaper. It is Rabindranath who introduced Lalon Fakir through his beautiful Baul songs to the lovers of the literary world. The following song became very popular:

Everyone asks what caste Lalon belongs to

Lalon says his observation failed to notice any colour of caste.

Rabindranath's favourite song was:

Khachar Vetor Ochin Pakhi Kamne Ase Jai

Rabindranath also did the English translation of this song.

In 1925, as the Chief Guest of the Bharatiya Philosophy Congress, he shared the English translation of the song with the audience.

'Nobody can tell whence the bird unknown comes into the cage and goes out.'

It may be mentioned that Rabindranath was the first person to translate the song into English for this great mystic saint. Subsequently, several Indian and foreign authors have translated the songs of Lalon into English, Hindi, French, German and Japanese.

During his stay in Shilaidaha, Rabindranath came into contact with several other mystic Baul singers, and he collected some of their songs.

It is worth mentioning that during that time, no village by the name of Shilaidaha existed in Kustia. Close to the cottage where Rabindranath stayed in Kustia, there was a swamp (daha) by the name of 'Shelly Sahib's Daha'. Poet Rabindranath named it Shilaidaha. Mahatma Lalon Fakir used to stay in the nearby village of Cheuria. Rabindranath had deep respect for Mahatma Lalon Fakir throughout his life.

GAGAN HARKARA

ONE DAY, sitting in his Kusthia cottage. Rabindranath was writing when he suddenly heard a beautiful voice singing a mystic Baul song:

Where would I find the person dear to my mind

I search around the world for that lost person.

My mind becomes sadly listless for that moonlight in my heart

If I could find that person, I would be overjoyed

I would be looking day and night with all my heart.

How can I diffuse the fume of sighs from the burning of love

candles.

Alas I am dying.

Come and see the pangs of pain from this separation

By tearing apart my heart.

The world is happy with God's unparallel love

I feel satiated looking at this

But I am too small to really see it unfolding.

The person who has realised having seen this, is overwhelmed

Has abandoned the household,

Alas I am dying.

No one knows with what jugglery

That person steals my mind unnoticed and by sneering.

I lost everything but still couldn't find that person.

My heart doesn't carry any string of love

GAGAN HARKARA

Therefore, the person doesn't appear before me.
Gagan is dying to find out where that person resides
Alas I am dying.
Oh, if you know that person's whereabout
I beg you to let me know.
My well-wisher and sufferer of the same pain as mine
Please tell me where to find that person.

Rabindranath listened to this song with rapt attention. The words of the spiritual song were simple, but deep and beautiful in meaning, and sung in such a melodious voice, that it excited and inspired the poet. He quickly came down from his upstairs room. He saw a mystic devotee dressed like a Baul, singing this song with the help of a one stringed instrument (*ektara*).

Rabindranath, with due respect, invited this singer to his house. Rabindranath introduced himself to this composer, musician and Baul singer. He was well known as Gagan Harkara (post man). He wrote his own songs and also composed the music for it. At Rabindranath's request, he again sang the song. Rabindranath, himself being a song writer, composer, and artist, appreciated with all his heart the marvelous impact of the language, the musical note and the feelings conveyed.

He discussed the inner meaning, the feelings expressed by the lyrics, and the tune of Baul songs with this mystic saint. In this way, Rabindranath collected a lot of information about Baul songs from Gagan. The undiminished, unmanifested Brahma of the Vedanta, the manifested form of atma, the representation of the Brahma of the Upanishads, the *paramatma* of Yoga, and the God of the devotee (Bhakti)—all of these exist as one, as inner being (*moner manush*), in the rich reservoir of the soul. Once you perceive this eternal great lover within you, the separation anxiety will cease to exist. Universal nectar exists within the treasury of the body. That is why you need outer body experience through this body only. Thereby, you experience the unification of a changeless lover person with the manifested entity when you become one within your *atma* (soul).

For this, one doesn't need to go to a temple or mosque. No outside ritual is necessary, only internal introspection is necessary. Just dive deep into the beautiful inner sea to find the great treasure – inner being (*moner manush*).

That is why the Bauls do not discriminate between the caste and the creed. They are a very liberal enlightened group of great humanity. They accept equally both Hindus and Muslims.

The sweet unification of Vedantic and Sufi thoughts has resulted in the Baul philosophy. They express the intense desire of the soul metaphorically to their dear *moner manush* in the lotus of their heart. He is sitting, simple and beautiful, in the midst of everybody.

Therefore, in Baul thought, simplicity is beautifully expressed.

The Baul devotees are bathed in the perception that divinity is present within humans and the devotees reside in a higher sphere, beyond this world and life.

Rabindranath felt an unfathomable attraction towards this world-oblivious and thoughtful Baul saint Gagan Bhattacharya.

Rabindranath in subsequent years, being inspired by the famous song and tune of Gagan Bhattacharya 'Where would I find the person dear to my mind,' he composed the song 'My golden Bengal, I love you. Always your sky, your air play like a flute in my soul'.

This song became a great source of inspiration for Bengal's national movement and later on when East Bengal was liberated from Pakistan, this song became the National Anthem for the country named 'Bangladesh'.

Thus, in this world, Rabindranath laid claim to the distinction of writing national anthems for two countries, India and Bangladesh.

Rabindranath, being a lover of Baul culture, happily declared himself again and again as Rabindra Baul. One can definitely point out that behind Rabindranath's worldwide fame and recognition, there was some contribution from this relatively unknown person from Bengal, Gagan Bhattacharya, the postman.

Normally, Rabindranath used to compose the tune of the song first and then incorporate the words into it. This practice was corroborated by Hemlata Tagore in her autobiography. It is apparent that if Rabindranath did not hear and accept this melodious and pleasantly distracting serene Baul (folk) song, he would have failed to create the immortal song 'My golden Bengal, I love you.' Had this song not been written, the Bengalis would have been deprived of a literary treasure. For this, every Bengali person along with Rabindranath, will remember with sincerity the contribution of this relatively unknown Baul, Gagan Bhattacharya.

The meeting place of these two great artists at Shilaidaha, will also be ever remembered by Bengalis.

When Rabindranath wanted to hear one more song written by Gagan Harkara himself, Gagan sang the following song with the help of a one string instrument (ektara):

How long will your mind

Remain absorbed in vain attachment

Where will you go

Watching the hoax that no one is for you.

You are fooling around the globe day and night

In search of the elixir of happiness

Still, you end up always unhappy.

When will you find the path of happiness?

For whom you are devoting life and fortune

Hoping they are close to you

No one will be with you

The day you leave this empty world.

Think about who is dearest to your soul

Who would sever this earthly bond

My aspired human life then

Would fade away this way, contemplates Gagan.

Listening to this song, Rabindranath experienced deep happiness within. Later, based on the tune of this song, Rabindranath composed the following song:

Whoever leaves you
I will not leave you, mother.
I will take refuge in your feet, mother
I will not care for anyone else.
Who says your home is poor?
Your heart is full of treasures.
I know how immensely valuable it is
I will not seek caress from others, mother.
Let others die for fame here and abroad
I will not forget mother your hand stitched bed sheet laid out
for me.
Wealth prestige try to distract me
My worries linger, mother
Rest assured; I will never bow to craze.

Anyway, Rabindranath learnt a lot from Gagan Bhattacharya about the personal lives and work of these mystic Bauls. The Bauls reached elevated levels in the spiritual field, but in their real life, they were engaged in low-income occupations and filled the lowest ranks of the social ladder. Some were cobblers, masons, carpenters, and farmers. Gagan Bhattacharya worked as a postman for a salary of just three rupees. Noticing this vast difference between their earthly and spiritual existence, Rabindranath was struck with awe. The dirtiness of the earthly living condition didn't have any impact sons the spiritual development of these mystic devotees. Rabindranath realised that this was possible because their hearts were always filled with deep spiritual knowledge and the fragrance of divine nectar.

Through Gagan Bhattacharya, Rabindranath met several other Bauls, such as Sarat Baul, Fakir Chand, Sheikh Madan Fakir, and others. Rabindranath collected many Baul songs from them. In the introduction of the book *Haramoni* (Folk and Baul songs assembled and edited by Md. Mansuriddin), Rabindranath wrote: 'People who follow my writings will know about my interest in Baul *padabalee* (collectionof songs) that I expressed in my writings several times. When I stayed in Shilaidaha, I was very close to the Bauls, and we had discussions on various topics.'

The influence of Baul songs and music was reflected in Rabindranath's songs, writings, and plays. He even acted as a Baul in one of his plays.

He wrote Baul songs on several occasions. The wordings and tunes wonderfully blended with the Baul tradition such as:

(1) *I keep my ears alert on the door of my own heart – many times*
     To listen to the secret whispering of words of tears and laughter
     – many times.
     Where the wandering bee is enjoying the nectar from a hidden
     lotus flower.
     Who is that night bird singing alone in the dark -many times.
     How it is related to me, nobody knows, I can perceive little
     of that light.
     I can perceive a little through imagination, some of it I
     cannot understand.
     Once in a while its message expressing my language into words,
     It sends me its wisdom disguised as a wording of the song
     – many times.

(2)   *My innermost one resides in me,*
      And He seems omnipresent hence.
      He rests within my eyes,
      I need not search for him at all –
      Whichever direction I look at –
      He seems within sight, hence.
      Traveling distances, in vain, for my wish –
      To listen to your sapient words,
      On home coming I find, thus,
      Lyrics of my songs having your words,
      You knock doors in frenzy
      In order to search Him-
      O' rush at me, look at my core,
      How He resides between my eyes.

In this way, immersed in Baul philosophy, Rabindranath composed several Baul songs with typical Baul tunes, such as:

I am looking for that person who resides in my
mind.
I know him, I know him, the person who
considers me close.
He is my inner being, why do you keep him
waiting at the door of my eyes.
My mind when you didn't wake up.
I know, I know that in your love permeates the
message of all love.
With what light you ignite the lamp of life and
come down to earth.

The wind is touching the sailboat of songs.
Mind O mind, you are the treasure of which
Sadhana.
When I remained blind…
Who wants to take me brother, I want to
surrender to you.
Your open breeze on the sail cuts it into pieces.
My joy lies in watching the days go by
Who is the mad man who is going from
neighborhood to neighborhood driving me crazy.

Rabindranath not only looked within for the inner being, but he also perceived the Divine within nature and His creation. Perceiving the Baul in the nature, the beauty of the rain, he composed a song as follows:

The cloud-Baul plays the one string instrument (ektara) all
day long like drizzles of rain.
It plays in the forests of berries and paddy fields in its own
merriment and dancing ecstasy.
Dark clouds form in the middle of the sky
Rain droplets pour making the sweet musical sound of anklets
on the feet.
Leaving the house in desperation and without hope
The east wind wanders around the homeless.

Also observing nature's beauty in the scarlet road beyond the village, it awakened the Baul spirit in him, and he happily composed the following wonderful song:

My King's road that lies still before my house makes my heart
wistful.
It stretches its beckoning hand towards me; its silence calls me
out of my home; with dumb entreaties.
it kisses my feet at every step.
It leads me on I know not to what abandonment, to what
sudden gain or surprises of distress.
I know not where its windings end-
But my King's road that lies still before my house makes my
heart wistful.
(Translated from Bengali by Rabindranath Tagore himself)

Later Rabindranath, dressed up as a Baul, with the single string instrument (*ektara*) acted in his own play and sang this song. His playing the role and singing the song became an instant success.

Rabindranath was very much impressed by Baul philosophy, its intense feeling and mystic worship of the formless inner self as lover. Their worship of humanity, truth and love affected Rabindranath's inner self. He could deeply feel the ever-pensive Baul within himself. That is why he projected himself as Rabindra Baul. Though leading a family life, he was very lonely. He was deeply pained at not getting the things he wanted. In his long life he moved around as a lonely Baul with his one string instrument and might have sung in melancholy pointing to his inner self the following:

Where will I find that person
Who is my inner self.

RAMANANDA BHARATI

THE PURSUIT of Indian spirituality from different corners namely Brahmo, Vaishnav, Shakta, Shaiva etc. have mingled gloriously in Swami Ramananda Bharati's life. Swami Ramananda was famous all over India as an erudite, reputed writer, a traveller, orator, spiritually powerful pursuer of truth, a great Yogi, and an austere religious practitioner.

Young Rabindranath first saw him at his father's residence. Ramananda used to come to the Jorasanko Thakurbari to exchange ideas on spirituality and the evolution of the Brahmo religion with Maharshi Debendranath. Rabindranath slowly got attracted to Ramananda during this period. Ramananda hadn't accepted renunciation (Sannyasi) yet. At that time his name was Ramkumar Bhattacharya aka Ramkumar Vidyaratna. He was very dear to Maharshi Debendranath. On Maharshi's instruction, he travelled to North Bengal, Orissa, and Assam in an effort to spread the Brahmo faith. While staying in Assam, he noticed the inhuman torture perpetrated by the British on tea garden coolies. In protest an indignant Ramkumar Vidyaratna wrote his immortal book *Cooli*. Later that book was translated into English and published as *Rice and Riot*.

As a result of the publication of this book, there was a revolt both inside and outside the country. The then Viceroy was forced to bring a law to end the torture inflicted upon coolies.

RAMANANDA BHARATI

Young Rabindranath developed deep respect for Ramkumar Vidyaratna after reading this book. At that time Ramkumar, who was busy in Calcutta on his mission to spread the Brahmo faith, visited Maharshi Debendranath.

Rabindranath was highly impressed with Ramkumar after conversing with him. Ramkumar's love for the motherland struck a chord in Rabindranath's mind. The urge, arising out of love for motherland, found expression in young Rabindranath's writing in the following poem:

All of you cry out "Oh my mother",

Let it soothe the ears of the rest of the world.

Let Himalaya's rock melt away by tears.

And you look at me by raising your face.

Let me see you all stand up by forgetting your self-interest.

Raising crores head at dawn's light

When twenty crores call out mother in unison

When twenty crores protect mother from all sides

That morning will usher in a new garden.

This is neither a story nor a dream.

When you cry out for your own mother

All sins and injustices will be swept away far.

God's blessing will shine.

By shaking off insults, the human spirit will rise.

Let thunder crisscross one heart to other.

Sing aloud without fear.

The infinite universe will be thrilling.

Happiness will smile all around.

A new life will be planted.

Sure, that day will come.
If you keep your brother close to your heart,
And when love stream flows,
There exists no tension, no sadness,
Only unblemished talent flourishes.

With the help of this song, Rabindranath, when he was a 24-year-old youth, expressed the anguish of subjugated Indians and their aspiration towards independence. In the year 1886, Rabindranath wrote another patriotic poem dedicated to the motherland:

Oh mother, why are you looking up to them.
They do not want you because they do not know their
own mother.
They are not going to assist you, no they will not – only
on the pretext they are telling you lies.
You are gifting away all you have - golden crops, flowing
Ganga River,
Knowledge, religion and so many holy stories.
What are they going to give you! Nothing! They tell only
lies from their inferior heart.
Mother, hide your grief inside your mind, don't let your
tears drop from your eyes.
Cover your face by lying on the dusty floor – forget your
all-unworthy sons.
See if you can spend the long night by vacant staring.
Mother, what will you gain by expressing your suffering
to cruel soulless stone-hearted beings.

One can only realise how much burning patriotism

Rabindranath felt inside him that he lashed out in rebuke through his song, to his callous and indifferent compatriots, men and women, immersed in luxury.

In the beginning of his life, Ramkumar Vidyaratna, assisted, as a writer cum scholar, for some time Michael Madhusudan in Chandannagore. Keshab Sen, Bijoykrishna Goswami, Shibnath Shastri and others had great affection for Ramkumar for his writing ability and oratory. Before accepting the Brahmo religion, Ramkumar married Sri Ramkrishna Paramhansa's blessed tantrik, Kotrang resident, Achalananda's daughter Gyanodadevi. After the marriage, Ramkumar with his wife and father-in-law went to Sri Ramkrishna at Dakshineshwar to offer *pronam* (reverence).

Since Ramkumar had accepted the Brahmo faith sometime after marriage, father-in-law Achalananda cut off all relations with him. Achalananda kept his daughter Gyanoda in his own house. During this time, Maharshi Debendranath gave shelter to Ramkumar at his house. This enhanced Rabindranath's proximity to this famous patriot.

Thereafter Ramkumar Vidyaratna with the help of his friend Shibnath Shastri brought his wife to his place. The family started living in Cornwallis street. After giving birth to three daughters, Gyanodadevi passed away in the year 1888.

In 1890, all of a sudden, Ramkumar renounced the Brahmo faith and accepted Hinduism from a holy person of the Bharati sect. He became known as Ramananda Bharati. His only worldly bondage was his three daughters. He kept his eldest daughter Susoma in a Brahmo boarding school for girls.

His distinguished Brahmo friend, the reputed writer

Upendrakishore Raychaudhuri (grandfather of world-famous film director Satyajit Roy), took charge of his second daughter. Friend Shibnath Shastri took charge of the youngest daughter Roma.

In the year 1891, Ramkumar received blessings from the Mahayogi and Mahatantrik Sri Sri Bamakhyapa when he visited the famous *satipitha* and ancient *tantrapitha* at Tarapith. Thereafter, Ramkumar blessed and initiated many devotees at Hazaribagh, Ranchi, Ramgarh, Almora, Kashi etc.

He subsequently participated in the Kumbh Mela at Haridwar. From there he set out on foot to the inaccessible pilgrimage site of Badrinath. He was accompanied by writer Jaladhar Sen and Achyutananda. Jaladhar Sen in his book *Himalay*, gave a lovely description of this journey.

After visiting holy abodes like Gangotri, Yamunotri, Gomukh, Kedarnath etc, Ramkumar visited on foot the highly inaccessible Mount Kailash, abode of Lord Shiva, and the lake Mansarovar in Tibet in 1898.

He is the first Bengali writer and traveller who on foot visited these remote sites dear to the Hindus, that lay in Tibet. In his written book *Himaronyo*, a delightful description of this journey is recorded.

Ramananda Bharati left his body at Kashi in the year 1901 at the age of sixty-five. His sacred body was encapsulated in a stone box by his disciples and drowned in the depths of the Ganges River.

When the news of his passing away reached Calcutta, the Brahmo fraternity was overcome with sadness and grief.

His Brahmo friends, including 84-year-old Maharshi Debendranath and forty-year-old Rabindranath paid respect to this immortal soul.

BHUPENDRA SANYAL

THE CELEBRATED Yogacharya and omniscient personality Bhupendranath Sanyal was the worthy disciple of Yogiraj Shyamacharan Lahiri, who was respected all over India. At the age of only sixteen years and five months, on 23 June 1893, Bhupendranath received initiation from the Yogiraj.

Within two years of initiation, Bhupendranath completed the full course of *Kriya* yoga and attained the next state of being. As a result of this attainment, Yogiraj Lahiri Mahashay gave Bhupendranath, who had already achieved enlightenment by *Kriya* yoga, the rare permission to initiate others into this practice. To be recognised as a spiritual guru at such an early age, was a rare accomplishment in India's history of yoga sadhana.

Under an unusual circumstance in 1903, world famous poet Rabindranath became acquainted with 26-year-old Bhupendranath in Shantiniketan.

Prior to this, Bhupendranath had visited an ailing 86-year-old Maharshi Debendranath and given a discourse in spirituality. Overjoyed Maharshideb told him, 'My dear son, the person who comes to a dying person and talks about God is the true friend. I am nearing death. Who could be a more useful friend than you who comforted me in God's name?'

In 1903, 42-year-old Rabindranath very earnestly

YOGACHARYA BHUPENDRANATH SANYAL

requested the 26-year-old enlightened yogi Brahmin who had been spiritually enriched with Vedic education, to accept full responsibility for running the brahmachari ashram.

After some time, Bhupendranath accepted Rabindranath's sincere request and took over all the duties of the ashram. Over time, he became principal of the ashram.

At that time Rabindranath was mentally anguished. Only a few months ago, his wife Mrinalini Devi had passed away (20 November 1902). Rabindranath lost his wife at the young age of 41. The entire responsibility of bringing up his children fell on his shoulders.

During that time, Rabindranath, drowning in depression, wrote a superb, deeply spiritual song.

> *There is grief, there is death, you feel the churning of separation.*
> *Yet peace and happiness reign in eternity.*
> *Life flows unabated, sun, moon and stars keep shining,*
> *Spring brightens the woods in varied hues.*
> *Waves play tide and web,*
> *Petals fall out as the flowers bloom.*
> *There is no destruction, no ending, not a speck of misery— My mind takes refuge at the feet of that Completeness.*

The great poet, through this great song painted the undying nature and face of eternity which symbolises our life force. The poet literally tried to unite the human soul, liberated from this temporary worldly suffering, with the blissful supreme spirit.

From 1903 to 1910, Rabindranath remained in close contact with the yogacharya Bhupendranath Sanyal.

Then, in agreement with Bhupendranath, Rabindranath started building a *brahmachari* ashram in accordance with the strict guidelines laid down for the establishment of an education ashram in the ancient mould.

Rabindranath tried to instill the same ideal practices that *brahmacharis* used to perform in ancient India, like taking care of the Guru, studying, cooking, and doing everything by themselves.

For that purpose, three potentially capable students were picked up by Rabindranath and Bhupendranath. They were prepared to be initiated into *brahmacharya* (the first stage of a traditional Hindu life) by Rabindranath, Bhupendranath and Mohit Sen.

The three students were Rabindranath's son Rathindranath, Saroj Chandra and Santosh Chandra.

At the right time, Rabindranath initiated Santosh Chandra, as did Bhupendranath Saroj Chandra, Mohit Sen, Rathindranath.

Close spiritual company and a *satsang* ambience was created for this purpose. Till 1909, this ideal atmosphere was maintained in all its glory. But after seven years of hard work, Bhupendranath's health broke down and he ultimately recused himself from the responsibility of running the ashram.

Later Bhupendranath gave *Kriya* yoga initiation to many men and women in Puri where he set up his ashram at Mandar.

He authored many books. He maintained a close relationship with Rabindranath till the end. Rabindranath viewed him with immense respect. Rabindranath often visited Bhupendranath to discuss spritiual matters. Rabindranath was particularly keen in knowing about *Kriya* yoga. Bhupendranath shared the depth of that practice with him. Later, Rabindranath was initiated into *Kriya* yoga by the world famous Buddhadeb Bose, disciple of Bhupendranath. It will be explained at the proper place. For seven long years, Rabindranath had a spiritual connection with Bhupendranath and both treasured that pleasant experience throughout their lives.

Even if your achievement is minimal, still go on practicing your sadhana. You must continue your practice. Although you may not presently feel the benefits, when the time is right, you will reap the rewards.

-Bhupendranath Sanyal

IDEAL MONK

WORLD POET Rabindranath was visiting Kashi (Benaras). This great city of pilgrimage, oldest in the world, was the abode for many monks and sages. Rabindranath was always in search of meeting holy people.

At that time, Rabindranath's very dear friend, Yogacharya Bhupendranath Sanyal, was residing in Kashi. Rabindranath asked Bhupendranath to introduce him to Sadhus since Kashi was the residing place for so many of them. Yogacharya smiled and said, 'Do you want to see the one whom I recognise as a *sadhu*?' Rabindranath joyfully replied, 'Yes I would like to meet him whom you recognise as a *sadhu*.'

Yogacharya Bhupendranath who had himself attained religious perfection, took Rabindranath to *siddha yogi* Krishnaramji, worthy disciple of *Yogiraj* Shyamacharan Lahiri.

At that time, Krishnaramji was residing at Ranamahal, Kashi. Rabindranath visited him there. For a while he discussed spiritual subjects with Krishnaramji. Bhupendranath also joined in the discussion.

Rabindranath, having come into contact with this enlightened Yogi, felt mentally satiated and happy. He understood the different path and meaning of India's yoga sadhana from Krishnaramji.

He acknowledged his hearty appreciation of both Krishnaramji and Bhupendranath.

KASHI (BENARAS)

PEAK OF TANTRISM

DHARMANANDA BHARATI was altogether a Siddha *Tantrik*, very wise, a good writer, traveller and proficient in many languages. Based on direct experience and realisation, he wrote several famous books on *Tantra Shakti* and *Mantra Shakti* in both English and Bengali languages. He wrote many articles in the *Hindusthan Spiritual Magazine* (1902-1922). Rabindranath was a regular reader of that magazine. As a result, Rabindranath came into contact with him and developed a close relationship through conversation. Rabindranath was, at the time, editing the *Bangadarshan Patrika* (1906-1910). He published many articles written by Dharmananda Bharati in this Patrika. Besides this, *Bharati Patrika* used to publish regularly articles by Dharmananda Bharati. Different facets of yoga (*swarodoy yoga, tantrik drishtiyoga, alok yoga*) were discussed in those articles. His famous book in English is *Tantricks and Tantrism*. Rabindranath was highly impressed with this book. While discussing *Tantrik Yoga* one day with Rabindranath, Dharmananda informed him that the famous *Tantrik* Khutkhute baba of Etawah was Dharmananda's guru. This guru had a meditation cave in Gujarat and had reached perfection in yoga and tantra practices. His supernatural power was witnessed by hundreds of his devotees.

He informed Rabindranath that he had come into contact

FAMOUS TANTRA SHRINE

with many famous saints. Among them were Mahayogi Onkardeo baba, Yogini Mataji, Shobhakar Bhattacharya, tantrik Gunapati Swami. Dharmananda Bharati travelled all over India. He had even been to Afghanistan, Sri Lanka and Singapore and had met with persons who had attained religious perfection and witnessed their miraculous spiritual feats. Rabindranath enriched himself highly in spirituality through his close relations with Dharmananda Bharati and that relationship lasted till the end.

NIVEDITA

WHEN HE first met her, Rabindranath hadn't realised the extent to which Sister Nivedita, an ascetic and a revolutionary, would embody the ideals and the spiritual teachings of Swami Vivekananda. Rabindranath readily accepted this when he wrote 'When I first met sister Nivedita, she had just arrived in India only a few days back. I thought she was like any other English missionary, the only difference being her religion was independent.'

With this false assumption on Nivedita in mind, Rabindranath asked her to teach his elder daughter Madhuri. The 31 year-old Nivedita rejected this request from 37 year-old Rabindranath outright. She said 'What is the utility in forcing a foreign culture? I consider that teaching to be perfect which arouses nationalistic skill and individual talent. I do not think it is fair to suppress that by thrusting a foreign education bound by certain rules.'

Swami Vivekananda's spiritual daughter, sister Nivedita, implemented this nationalistic ideal, in the school that she established. Rabindranath, later witnessing this, developed an immense respect for her. Observing Nivedita's devotion to her Guru and gradually transforming herself into an Ideal Bengali, thoroughly Indian in her outlook, impressed him highly.

Nivedita grasped India's spiritual wealth by reading the

SISTER NIVEDITA

Vedas, Vedanta, Upanishads, the Puranas, the Ramayana, the Mahabharata, the Gita, the Chandi, Patanjali's Yoga darshan, Sankhya Darshan, etc. and completely assimilated all these texts. She distilled the essence of all these branches of spiritual knowledge and inculcated that as the ideal to follow in her school. About this ideal education, she mentioned that, 'The imagined basis for the children of this nation should be the Ramayana and the Mahabharata. One doesn't become great immediately after being born. A soul is nurtured to become great by strong thoughts. Every person has a desire for self-giving. Education fosters that longing. Then only the nationalistic ownership awakens.'

Rabindranath deeply realised the meaning of education from this comment of Sister Nivedita. As a result, Rabindranath's educational system at Santiniketan reflects Nivedita' s ideology.

Under the spell of a spiritual trance, Rabindranath, looking at the vast expanse of Santiniketan, wrote a memorable song that unfolded with pride the true spiritual education bestowed on this institution situated in the lap of nature.

> *In this great universe under the great sky, in the middle*
> *of time*
> *I am human alone, in delusional wonder.*
> *You are here Vishwanath, in the infinite mystery,*
> *Silently alone in your world of glory.*
> *In this eternal country, under countless shining areas*
> *You are present staring at me, me staring at you.*
> *All the noise silenced; peace has engulfed the land.*
> *You are alone, in your midst I am alone, fearless.*

The year is 1905. The turmoil of the first partition of Bengal partition had commenced. The whole country burst out in protest against this proposed partition. Rabindranath wrote a series of patriotic songs to inspire the masses. These powerful lyrics almost set fire to Bengali emotions. He continued writing songs one after another dedicated to the motherland:

Where from our heart, did you emerge Mother
Bengal….
Whoever may leave you, I will not leave you…
I will not fear, will not fear…
Now water current has resumed in your dry land…
You cannot worry thinking someone will leave you….
If nobody responds to your call, walk alone…

Vivekananda's blessed disciple, sister Nivedita, used to give lectures every Thursday at the Brahmo society despite her many-sided work schedule. Ladies affectionate towards Rabindranath, regularly visited Nivedita to listen to her lectures. Mentionable among those ladies were, Rabindranath's niece Indira Chaudhurani, the two daughters, viz. Sunitidevi and Sucharudevi of Brahmo leader Keshab Chandra Sen, the editor of *Bharati Patrika*, Srijukta Sarala Ghosal, Acharya Jagadish Chandra Bose's sister Labonyaprobha Bose and others.

In the year 1904, sister Nivedita visited Bodhgaya with a group of people that included Rabindranath, Acharya Jagadish Chandra Bose with his wife, Vivekananda's co-worker Swami Saradananda, sister Christine, Swami Sankarananda, Samuel Ratcliffe with his wife and others.

Everyone spent some pleasant days at this sacred pilgrimage site. They enjoyed discussing spiritual subjects, literary books, and music.

In this grand spiritual atmosphere, Rabindranath, having come into close contact with Nivedita, realised that she was an ascetic and completely devoted to the teachings of Sri Ramkrishna Paramhansa and Swami Vivekananda. Very frequently Nivedita used to talk about her recently published book *The Aim of Indian Life* and about her Guru Swami Vivekananda and supreme Guru Sri Ramkrishna. At that time, she wrote another famous book *The Master as I Saw Him*. Everyone present was delighted when Nivedita read out of this book.

After returning from Bodhgaya, Rabindranath invited sister Nivedita to visit Shilaidaha. He also invited Jagadish Chandra Bose. Nivedita reached Shilaidaha, accompanied by Jagadish Bose right on time in December 1904. Nivedita felt very good amidst the quiet natural beauty of the river Padma. Due to relentless hard work, her health had also broke down by then.

Despite her broken health, she was following the ideal and instruction of Swamiji to the letter. She was reminded quite often about Swamiji's godly memories. She often recited from the book *Kali the Mother* written by Swamiji.

Swamiji's complete devotion to and taking refuge under Ma Kali, the universal mother, was a beacon to Nivedita.

Nivedita recalled an incident at Amarnath in Kashmir.

One day Swamiji told Nivedita 'Do meditation for death. Worship the destroyer of evil, Ma Kali. She is the embodiment of universal strength.'

Another day, 5 November 1899, during Swamiji's second trip to the west, he was travelling to New York and Nivedita was on her way to Chicago to arrange funds for Belur Math. Before she started her journey, Vivekananda advised her, 'All the time, keep saying in your mind Durga, Durga. This will save you from danger.'

All of a sudden Swamiji rather excitedly yet firmly blurted out, 'Not just prayer. She has to be forced to fulfill that. No begging in a lowly manner to Mother will do.'

Another incident took place in October 1900, when Swamiji wrote from Paris to Nivedita, 'You are independent. Likes and dislikes are your own choice. Your work will also be accordingly. Both friend and enemy are the instruments of Mother. With their help, Mother, both in times of distress and happiness, gets our work done. That is how She showers her kindness on all of us .'

On another occasion, he told Nivedita, 'Kali, Kali, Kali. She is in presence, she is the change, she is the infinite strength. Her presence is always in the heart of those who are fearless. Where there is sacrifice, selflessness, readiness to embrace death by all means—there is the presence of Ma.'

After returning from Khir Bhabani in Kashmir, the Vedantic Swami Vivekananda, absorbed in absolute meditation, said to Nivedita, 'Whatever you see, is the reflection of Ma. Everyone is good – we just don't have the capacity to accept everyone.'

All these godly statements Nivedita remembered during her stay at Shilaidaha. She stated some of these to Jagadish Bose and Rabindranath. Both were mesmerised, listening to her.

Though Rabindranath was a believer of Brahmo, he had no dogmatism about other religions.

He was completely open-minded about different paths and opinions of all other religions.

He himself said, 'Though I was born in a Brahmo family, my mind has no superstition about worshipping God.' Later in his life, it was noticed that Rabindranath had developed an enormous respect for different sects of Hindu religion like Shakta, Shaiva, Brahma, Vaishnav, etc. In particular, he was so much respectful of Vaishnav literature and the Vaishnav way of meditation, that he wrote to his distinguished friend, Acharya Brajendra Sil, classmate of Swami Vivekananda, that 'my mental aptitude has been formed out of mingling of Vaishnav literature and the Upanishads. It is almost like mixing oxygen and nitrogen in the air.'

About the central force of Vaishnav religion, Sri Chaitanya Mahaprabhu, Rabindranath very respectfully wrote, 'Like emotion, so was his voice. The crying sound is the result of sweeping tears and bringing everyone together. I feel proud of this unique talent of Bengal's kirtan music. This religious love of Chaitanyadev is of high standard and spotless.'

Rabindranath also had great respect for the poets dedicated to spirituality in Vaishnav religion and literature. In particular he translated into English from Bengali and Hindi, the writings of medieval poets like Gyandas, Chandidas, Vidyapati, Dadu Kabir and others.

It is unknown to many that Rabindranath had gathered Kabir's dohas through Khitimohan Sen and translated it into English, a translation that was later published from London.

In this context, a letter from the world poet Rabindranath, while staying in America, is memorable. He wrote from America to Khitimohan Sen, 'From the Middle Ages, whatever documents about India's mystics are available, you will need to collect and assemble. Collect as much as possible the writings of Dadu Kabir, Mirabai, Gyandas and others. Besides this, pick up Baul songs of Bengal as much as you can. To understand the heart of India, these are required. Bring our books that relate to dualism. Besides this, do not forget to collect the life story of Chaitanya and poems written by Vaishnav poets.'

Rabindranath expressed his great appreciation for Sri Sri Chaitanya Mahaprabhu—the heart and soul of the Vaishnav religion—in a letter to his dear son Rathindranath, 'Once Chaitanya made us Vaishnav. There is no caste in Vaishnav religion.' Elsewhere he wrote about the Mahaprabhu with great respect, 'Mahaprabhu mesmerised the whole world by chanting Hari Nam. He roused Indianness through this devotion to Hari.'

In Shilaidaha, Rabindranath was very happy in observing the incomparable motherly nature of sister Nivedita.

By visiting the poor peasants' homes, Nivedita listened with compassion to their stories of good and bad times.

Sister Nivedita was also very respectful of Rabindranath. That is why without any hesitation, she wrote about Rabindranath, 'He is perfect in his behavior. An easy aura of sense of dignity emanates from his conversation. However, his delivery in conversation is so simple, it touches your heart. Songs and humor are his constant companions. While he is prompt to please others, he is also happy within himself.'

Nivedita returned to Calcutta from Shilaidaha. But she kept in touch with Rabindranath.

Once Rabindranath made an offer to Nivedita. He wanted to give her a big paternal house. It was Rabindranath's wish that Nivedita establish her school in that house. But Nivedita very politely rejected that offer.

At that time Rabindranath was not in a good frame of mind. A procession of deaths went past him. Deaths of his family members hit him hard. He let his agony out by writing many songs at that time:

1. *When the purpose of life dries up, shower me with*
   kindness.
   When the pleasantness hides away, bring me musical
   nectar.
   When the work turns overwhelming by its thundering
   presence from all sides
   O' silent lord, reach on the edge of my heart in silent
   steps.
   By making myself miser, my poor inferior heart sulks
   in the corner
   Opening the door, O' my gracious lord, come in a
   royal charter.
   When the dust of desires blinds the ignorant,
   O' the sacred, O' the vigorous, show up in flashes of
   anger.

(Poem was written on 11 April 1910)

2. *O' dear, quiet the expressible poet now*

You play deep by snatching the flute within him.
Dip the flute in the symphony, mid of the night,
The tune that astonishes the moon and the planets.
Whatsoever of mine remains scattered in life and death,
Get them attracted to merge on your feet.
Loads of words would be washed away momentarily,
I will be listening to the flute all alone in the endless dark.

(Poem was written on 13 April 1910)

3. *I have to wash myself with your kindness,*
   Else will I ever be able to touch your feet?
   When I bring offerings in a platter, my blemishes show up,
   My heart, therefore, fails to rest at your feet.
   Till now I had no sense of regret within me
   Because I was covered in grime.
   Today my heart cries for those sacred arms
   Do not O' do not let me lie in the dust anymore.

(Poem was written 28 May 1910)

4. *I know that this life, missing its ripeness in love, is not*
   altogether lost.
   I know that the flowers that fade in the dawn, the
   streams that strayed in the desert, are not altogether lost.
   I know that whatever lags behind in this life laden
   with slowness is not altogether lost.

I know that my dreams that are still unfulfilled, and my melodies still unstruck, are clinging to some lute-strings of thine, and they are not altogether lost.

(Rabindranath Tagore translated this himself and therefore we copied his translation).

Poem was written on 7 August 1910)

Sister Nivedita's deep sense of spirituality, vast work commitment, concentration, erudition, exceptional knowledge, prowess, child-like simplicity, extreme love for the country, endless sacrifice earned great respect from Rabindranath.

At that time, Rabindranath translated his story *Kabuliwala* into English. He felt pleased after reading that.

Later Rabindranath paid respect to Nivedita by referring to her as *Lokmata* (people's mother). In his eyes, she embodied all the great qualities of a woman.

In the year 1911, in Darjeeling, this great ascetic lady left for her heavenly abode, aged only 44.

This illuminated divine lady, born in the distant town of Dungannon, Ireland in 1867, made her final peaceful resting place at the foothills of the sacred Himalayas after burning her tumultuous energy for 44 years for the sake of Mother India.

Sister Nivedita remains forever as a shining bridge between the east and the west by combining spirituality, literature, and love for motherland sourced from two cultures.

"Our daily life creates our symbol of God. No two ever cover quite the same conception".

— Sister Nivedita

PERFECTION IN SPIRITUALITY

MAHATMA BIJOYKRISHNA GOSWAMI came to see a very old Maharshi Debendranath at his home. The 87-year-old Maharshideb was awaiting the final call from heaven. Bijoykirshna Goswami had already been acclaimed all over India as someone who had attained perfection in spirituality. But to Maharshideb, he still remained the person he called 'Bijoy' with affection. This was quite natural. Since his student life, Bijoykrishna had been blessed with affection by Maharshideb. Since then, Bijoykrishna had been visiting Maharshideb for various reasons. There was a time when he was an active member and leader of the Brahmo community. With inspiration from Maharshideb, he switched over from the Hindu religion to the Brahmo one.

Later the Brahmo congregation split into three due to internal dissensions. Bijoykrishna, left the Maharshideb-run Adi Brahmo Samaj and joined the Keshab Sen-run Indian Brahmo Samaj. Later, Bijoykrishna formed the Sadharan Brahmo Samaj by joining hands with Shibnath Shastri and Anando Mohan Basu. Despite ideological differences, the private relationship between Maharshideb and Bijoykrishna never suffered a breakdown. Maharshideb's youngest son and editor of the Adi Brahmo Samaj publications, Rabindranath, noticed this all along. Rabindranath also always had a strong relation with Bijoykrishna.

BIJOYKRISHNA GOSWAMI

Later in life, Bijoykrishna Goswami, left Brahmo Samaj, and went back to the Hindu fold. After initiation from a guru, he became a sanyasi and practiced severe religious austerity. He was congratulated for achieving enlightenment by Sri Sri Ramdas Kathiababa, Sri Ramakrishna Paramhansa, Bhola Nanda Giri Maharaj, Swami Gambhirananda, Sri Sri Loknath Bramhachari and other distinguished Indian saints. He still had a very sincere and strong relationship with both Maharshideb and Rabindranath.

Maharshideb showed appropriate courtesy to Bijoykrishna. Maharshideb gladly embraced Bijoykrishna. At the Maharshi's request, Bijoykrishna started talking about spiritual matters. Hours passed by in reciting the divine name and song. The 87-year-old Maharshideb, absorbed in deep thought, conveyed his affection and love to Bijoykrishna. He profusely thanked Bijoykrishna, with tearful eyes, for the soothing divine discourse Bijoykrishna had delivered at the twilight of his life.

It is quite understandable to what heights Bijoykrishna ascended, from the respectful comments made by Indian saints with regard to Bijoykrishna, the real successor to the Advaita Mahaprabhu.

Sri Ramkrishna, God's incarnation, said, 'The room, if one can enter, he or she will attain perfection of religious austerity, Bijoy has reached the next room and knocking at the door.'

The person who reached the pinnacle of Indian spirituality, Mahatma Troilanga Swami said about Bijoykrishna Goswami 'This kid is all good.'

The great sadhu, famous all over India, Sri Sri Ramdas Kathia Baba, said about Bijoykrishna that, 'It is rare to find a Mahatma like Bijoykrishna.'

Mahayogi Bholananda Giri respectfully said about Bijoykrishna that, 'He can be pleased easily.' Not only that, as long as Bijoykrishna was alive, he didn't give initiation to any Bengali. He asked them to get initiated by Bijoykrishna.

Seeing happiness in the face of his aged father after listening to religious sermons from Bijoykrishna, Rabindranath also expressed his gratitude to Bijoykrishna. The degree of respect that Bijoykrishna held for a paternal figure like Maharshi Debendranath Tagore, can be evidenced from the following incident.

Once, a fierce argument erupted within the Brahmo Samaj about the appropriateness of calling Debendranath, Maharshi. One faction held that Debendranath being a family man, a very rich zamindar, and father of many children was too worldly to be called a Maharshi. The other faction retorted that despite all of the above, he was completely focused on God. Sri Ramkrishna, came on his own accord to Debendranath's home, had a spiritual discourse with Debendranath and then acclaimed him, 'the father of this age'. Therefore, it was appropriate to call him 'Maharshi'.

On this issue, when Bijoykrishna was asked about his opinion, he remained calm and said 'By calling him Maharshi, we aren't showing adequate respect to him. He deserves to be called 'Maha Maharshi' (over and above plain 'Maharshi)'. Hearing such an affirmation of faith coming from a famous spiritual person, the opposition was too stunned to react and was left speechless.

Mahatma Bijoykrishna, on the strength of his endless spiritual strength, was surely aware of Rabindranath's birth details as preordained by God. The Maharshi while staying in the foothills of the Himalayas, received a divine message about Rabindranath prior to his birth.

That is why Bijoykrishna had a brotherly love, affection, and respect for Rabindranath. Rabindranath also, always in search of great sages, remained highly respectful of Bijoykrishna till the end.

BAMAKHYAPA

RABINDRANATH was aware for quite some time of the mystic reputation of Sri Sri Bamakhyapa—a famous tantrik and Mahayogi of Mahapith Tarapith, Birbhum (West Bengal). In the year 1872, Rabindranath's father Maharshi Debendranath Tagore, visited Sri Sri Bamakhyapa at Tarapith and received his blessings. Rabindranath was only 11 years old then. It is probably unknown to many people that the person behind the establishment of Santiniketan ashram was Sri Sri Bamakhyapa, who had told Maharshideb, 'You are going to Sinha's (Lord S P Sinha) house at Raipur for a dinner invitation. On your way, you will find a huge dry land. In the middle, you will see a big Chatim tree. Sit below the tree and meditate. You will find peace by realising your illuminated inner self. Establish your ashram at that spot. You will achieve peace there.'

After meditating for quite a while under the tree, the Maharshi experienced an unearthly happiness and uninterrupted peace.

Later, on 22 December 1872 (in accordance with Brahmo spiritual practice), he set up under the Chatim tree, his ashram as per the advice from Bamakhyapa. Maharshideb's friend, Lord S P Sinha, donated this huge parcel of land with the Chatim tree for the purpose of building an ashram to the Maharshi. Upon special request, Lord Sinha accepted only 'one rupee' in

PARAMPURUSH SRI SRI BAMAKHYAPA

"The son who does not provide food for his old parents, wastes not only this life but hereafter"

exchange for the registration of this land. This ashram, later became known as Santiniketan, turned world famous through the effort of Rabindranath. Rabindranath must have surely heard this story from his father. Maharshideb affectionately blessed the well-known spiritual personality Ramkumar Vidyaratna, aka Ramananda Bharati who visited Bamakhyapa at Tarapith and received his blessing.

Rabindranath's close friend and the principal of Brahmacharya school at Santiniketan, *Kriyayogi* Bhupendranath Sanyal, visited Tarapith and received blessings from Bamakhyapa. Rabindranath, always in search of pious souls, must have been briefed by Bhupendranath about Bamakhyapa. Also, it is relevant here that Rabindranath met the enlightened soul Krishnaramji at Kashi when he was accompanied by Bhupendranath. It would not be out of the ordinary to suppose that Rabindranath on hearing so much about Bamakhyapa of Tarapith—only a two-hour-journey by train from Santiniketan, would be eager to meet him.

A middle-aged Rabindranath became very restless to meet Bamakhyapa. At this time, due to some family matters, he came to his Calcutta property at Jorasanko. While he was staying there, Mukunda Das, famous for composing ballads and being involved in the independence struggle, came to meet with Rabindranath at Jorasanko. Mukunda Das, a poet, musician and revolutionary was at that time a very popular name amongst Bengalis. In the middle of the conversation, Mukunda Das informed Rabindranath that he was going to meet Bamakhyapa at Tarapith, Birbhum and receive blessing from the saint.

Rabindranath was very pleased to hear this. He had the same desire in his heart. So, Rabindranath expressed his desire to Mukunda Das. He wanted to see this ancient pilgrimage site that combines both a *satipith* and a *tantrapith*, and its Mahayogi Bamakhyapa – the soul of Tarapith and a reflection of Lord Shiva. Mukunda Das was also pleased to know about Rabindranath's wish.

After a few days, both of them boarded the train at night for their Tarapith destination. Early in the morning, after reaching Rampurhat station, they crossed seven miles by bullock driven carriage to reach Tarapith. Entering Tarapith, Rabindranath and Mukunda Das were struck by the rather scary beauty of this ancient seat of Tantra.

On one side of Tarapith, there was the dense crematorium, on the other, a huge expanse of green crops. There was a red ochre walkway through the middle. Walking towards the south, they came across Bamakhyapa's outhouse—almost like a shed, and a living pond. After crossing that, they reached the temple of the mother goddess Tara. Paying respectful homage to the mother of three worlds of the universe (heaven, earth, and netherworld), they sat on the floor of the temple. They heard from the local priest that Bamakhyapa usually visited the temple during the feeding time of the idol. Sometimes he ate the prasad at the temple and at other times he did it at his own ashram. He was a free willed liberated person. Everything happened according to his wish. He wasn't present at his ashram at that time. No one knew where he was. Quite a few people were waiting at his ashram for his appearance.

Rabindranath and Mukunda Das decided to stay put at the temple and waited for Bamakhyapa's arrival. They waited for almost the entire day but didn't get to see the saint. Both of them felt discouraged. The local priest told them no one could know where Bamakhyapa was. At times, after crossing the Dwarka river on the west side of the crematorium, he would reach the Udaipur Kali temple by remaining afloat on his yogic power. Sometimes he would sit quietly at a hidden place near the crematorium. Other times, he would remain submerged in the living pond. As a result, the visitors had to wait for hours with endless patience. It also happened sometime a lucky visitor could meet him immediately on arrival at the temple or at his ashram.

Rabindranath and Mukunda Das kept on waiting at the temple patiently. Gradually dusk set in and yet there was no sign of Bamakhyapa. Both of them had travelled almost sleeplessly on the train and gone hungry and without a bath. The mental state of the duo could be easily understood. In the past, Rabindranath went to different places to visit saints but never had to wait for the entire day. Naturally, Rabindranath became restless. Mukunda Das was also depressed and was thinking of returning.

Tara Ma was affectionately staring at her two sons—one a great poet and the other a great revolutionary. These two persons were waiting timidly to meet Tara Ma's best son— godly figure among men, the Mahayogi, Lord Shiva's reflection in a true Brahmin Bamakhyapa.

Eventually, with the blessing of Tara Ma, Rabindranath

and Mukunda Das passed the test for patient waiting. All of a sudden, they both heard from a distance, a thunderous voice calling, Tara, Tara and Ma, Ma.

The surroundings trembled. It appeared as if someone was storming in by creating turmoil in the forest and the adjoining dwellings.

Both were overjoyed after hearing Bamakhyapa's thunderous voice and at the same time were frightened. The priest said, 'There comes Bamakhyapa.' Immediately, they saw a huge dark skinned very powerful person standing in front of them. It appeared as if powerful beams were radiating out from his blood shot eyes. He was wearing only a loincloth.

This huge lively individual glanced at them once and then went straight inside the temple and started sucking milk from the breast of Tara Ma's idol made of stone. Rabindranath and Mukunda Das were dumb struck watching this paranormal scene. They were stunned to see Bamakhyapa drinking heartily the milk and watched as the excess milk dripped down his mouth and cheeks.

After finishing the drink, suddenly Bamakhyapa asked them 'Where are you from?'

They both replied, 'We have come from Calcutta.'

Suddenly Bamakhyapa looked at Mukunda Das and said 'You are carrying a firearm. Go and immediately throw it away in the river.'

Mukunda Das, initiated in violent revolution, realised Bamakhyapa could know and see everything. In fact, Mukunda did carry a revolver with bullets on his person. In order to kill the enemy and for personal defense, revolutionaries were required to carry revolvers. In the past, Mukunda Das had served time in prison for his anti-British activities. Besides that, British spies were always following him. That is the reason he always kept the firearm with him. He was not willing to throw this in the water. At the same time, he felt that he couldn't defy an order of this powerful sage.

It is also to be noted here, that upon instruction from Bamakhyapa, two of his disciples, Mahatma Tarakhyapa and Ramnath Aghoribaba, joined the independence movement. Bamakhyapa's clear instruction was, 'The universal mother is the motherland. The shackles of the motherland have to be broken first. Unless the land is free, you cannot meditate independently.' More than one young revolutionary received blessings and shelter from him. The famous revolutionary and later enlightened soul, Swami Swarupananda Paramahansa was one of them.

Mukunda Das realised that it was not possible to defy the order of a person of that stature. He inferred that Bamakhyapa had given this order for his own overall good. Mukunda Das, in two minds, hesitantly got up. All-knowing Bamakhyapa saw this and ordered Rabindranath, 'You go with him and make sure he drops it.'

As per Bamakhyapa's order both left the temple and started walking towards the Dwarka river through the crematorium. They were surprised to see two black and white dogs (by the name Lalu and Bhulu, constant companions of Bamakhyapa) were following them.

Evening was approaching. Gradually darkness was engulfing the deep forest in the middle of the crematorium. Around the crematorium, human skeletons and dead bodies were scattered. Foxes and dogs were fighting over the half burnt and melted flesh. Side by side, venomous snakes were slithering past them. There was an eerie sound emanating from the wind passing through human skulls. Screeching cries from vultures were coming from a distance. Watching these terrifying scenes, Rabindranath and Mukunda Das reached the west end of the Dwarka river.

Mukunda Das dropped his favourite revolver in the river. Thereafter, both set out for the temple following the same path. The dogs also followed them. Surprisingly enough, nothing, not excluding all the scattered bones and skulls around the crematorium, touched their feet. There was no dedicated pathway in their journey, and they literally walked in almost darkness.

Finally, both made a safe return to the temple. Seeing them, kindhearted Bamakhyapa said, 'You are both hungry, right?'

Saying this, he picked up two clay pots hanging from a hook. He handed over the two pots to them.

Rabindranath and Mukunda Das were shocked to see that both the pots were covered by fungus. They were wondering how they were going to eat this strange item. However, watching a little while ago, the miraculous scene of Bamakhyapa drinking milk from the idol made of stone, they thought this item could be fit for consumption also. More so, because Bamakhyapa, out of kindness gave them to eat. With this thought, Mukunda

Das first tasted a bit of this liquid fungus with his finger. He was pleasantly surprised at the taste and flavor of the item. It was as if he had never eaten such a tasty item before. Happily, he said to Rabindranath, 'Are you still wondering? Eat it with full confidence.'

They both happily ate the entire food. Immediately, both of them felt satiated and reinvigorated. In the mind and the body, they felt strength and peace. At that time, Bamakyapa asked kindly, 'Why have you come to Tarapith? It is already dark now; you go away now, otherwise you will be in danger.'

Hearing this, Rabindranath and Mukunda Das got up to leave after touching the feet of Bamakhyapa. Suddenly Bamakhyapa said to Rabindranath, 'Listen, with Tara Ma's blessing, you will be famous in the world. You will be an ascetic and you will achieve enlightenment.' Saying this he blessed Rabindranath. Then he blessed revolutionary Mukunda Das and said, 'Tara Ma has given you strength for singing and writing. You serve your mother with those qualities. And remember the universal mother is no other than your motherland. At the proper time our land will be independent. The path you are following will bring forth independence. Shun the path of violence and dedicate yourself in the name of the mother. Good will happen to you and you will be a person of repute.'

Having received this blessing, both were overjoyed and took leave from Tarapith. They both walked in darkness through this seven-mile long unknown path and reached the Rampurhat station safely. Immediately the train arrived. They reached Bolpur after a two-hour ride. From there they reached Santiniketan by bullock-cart at night.

In later times, Bamakhyapa's predictions with regard to Rabindranath came to be hundred per cent true. Rabindranath became world famous by being awarded the Nobel Prize and Mukunda Das's name spread far and wide in the country.

Mukunda Das's nationalistic song, *With coarse cloth of your mother, cover your head brother* and other songs kindled sentiments of love for the motherland among crores of Bengalis.

It is worth mentioning here that during Rabindranath's wedding at the age of 24, the Mahayogi Bahera Baba had predicted that one day Rabindranath would be world famous. Bahera Baba also visited Bamakhyapa at Tarapith and fed him *payesh* (dessert made with rice, milk and sugar) with his own hand. It is also to be noted here that young Narendranath (later Swami Vivekananda) and his classmate Sarat Chakrabarti, had visited Bamakhyapa during their student days and the sage had blessed Narendranath, predicting the latter would spread the glory of Hindu religion all across the globe. After ten years, this prediction came true. Swami Vivekananda, as a representative of the Hindu religion, gave a memorable lecture at Chicago during a world conference of religions and became world famous. Therefore, in India's spiritual world, it was Bamakhyapa who first made the prediction about Swami Vivekananda.

The sweet memory of Bamakhyapa remained etched forever in the hearts of Rabindranath and Mukunda Das.

At this time Rabindranath was 45 years old, (year 1906)

and after returning from Tarapith, he authored this devotional song which was considered to be the first song of his book, *Geetanjali*. It is this book that brought the Nobel Prize for the poet.

This song exemplifies extraordinarily the triangular fusion of love, devotion, and resignation before the Almighty.

Lower my head below the dust under your feet.

Drown all my conceit in tears.

While gifting myself pride, I only insult myself,

Circling around myself over and over again

My journey ends in vain.

Drown all my ego in tears.

I should not be advertising myself through my own work

May your wishes be fulfilled in my life.

I seek your absolute peace, your splendor in my heart

You stand as a barrier in the lotus of my heart.

Drown all my conceit in tears.

RAMNATH AGHORIBABA

FAMILY PHYSICIAN Dr J M Dasgupta aka Jatindra Mohan Dasgupta knew that the world poet Rabindranath Tagore always sought the company of sadhus.

Dr Dasgupta was not only a great doctor, he was also known in India as a reputable politician.

He was a patriot and gathered respect as a President of the Bengal Congress. He was close to Deshbandhu Chittaranjan Das, and a favourite person with national political icons such as Mahatma Gandhi, Lokmanya Tilak, Bipin Chandra Pal, Lala Lajpat Rai and other all India leaders. He was very affectionate towards new leaders such as Pandit Jawaharlal Nehru and Subhas Chandra Bose. Lajpat Rai never failed to meet with Dr Dasgupta, and discussed many issues with him whenever he came to Bengal. It goes without saying that Deshbandhu Chittaranjan Das also used to join in the discussion. J M Dasgupta went to jail many times for the sake of the country. Rabindranath had a special affection for this person who was fearless, a follower of truth, patriotic and determined. It was not unknown to Rabindranath that J M Dasgupta travelled spiritually inside him beyond everyone's knowledge. Rabindranath realised this many times while talking to him. J M Dasgupta's Gurudev was the Mahayogi Sri Sri Ramthakur, famous all over India. India's sadhus who were on the path

YOGIRAJ RAMNATH AGHORIBABA

of spiritual perfection highly respected Sri Sri Ramthakur. His miraculous acts were known all over the country.

Being a favourite disciple of Sri Sri Ramthakur, Dr Dasgupta had witnessed for a long time the miraculous deeds of his master. He used to share those stories with Rabindranath. Rabindranath eagerly listened to those stories. Dr Dasgupta used to stay at Ballygunge Place in South Calcutta. The name of the house was Ramnivas where distinguished persons like Deshbanndhu Chittaranjan Das, Dr Sarvapalli Radhakrishnan—later President of India— littérateur Sarat Chandra Chattopadhyay and others visited Sri Sri Ramthakur. They all were blessed by Sri Sri Ramthakur.

Sarat Chandra Chattopadhyay was suffering from acute indigestion since long. He was treated by Dr Dasgupta. Knowing from Dr Dasgupta about Sri Sri Ramthakur, he expressed his desire to see the sage. At that time, Ramthakur was residing at Ramnivas. With Ramthakur's permission, Sarat Chandra visited the holy man and was very pleased. During the conversation, Ramthakur asked him to eat the prasad of the deity saying he would be relieved of his indigestion. Sarat Chandra felt encouraged after hearing this. Then during lunch one day, Sarat Chandra ate the prasad. He enjoyed it thoroughly. Within a few days Sarat Chandra was cured completely of his indigestion.

Sarat Chandra expressed his gratitude to Ramthakur by visiting him after a few days and offered his *pranam*. Ramthakur blessed him. Sarat Chandra remained deeply respectful towards Ramthakur till the end of his life.

When during the independence movement Dr Dasgupta, as Congress president went to jail, the British government offered him the post of Prime Minister of Bengal (during the undivided Bengal regime, the chief minister was referred to as prime minister). Dr Dasgupta rejected that offer. While he was in jail, Ramthakur with his disciples, among whom Deshbandhu Chittaranjan Das, built this house Ramnivas on a few acres of land at Ballygunge Place. At that time Ballygunge Place was a dense forest. Since at this place, big snakes used to hang from the trees, it was referred to as Cluster of snakes Parganas and that's what Dr Dasgupta told Rabindranath. This famous 'Ramnivas' was the first house to be built at Ballygunge Place. Rabindranath, always in search of meeting sadhus, expressed his desire to meet Ramthakur at this Ramnivas.

Dr Dasgupta found out that Sri Sri Thakur, at that time, was residing in Chaumohoni in East Bengal. Therefore, the meeting didn't take place. After some time, Sri Sri Thakur arrived in Calcutta. But at that time Rabindranath was abroad. As a result, the meeting didn't take place. Like this, three times Dr Dasgupta tried to arrange a meeting between the two, but due to some divine intervention, it didn't occur.

When Thakur reached Calcutta, Rabindranath was stationed outside. When Sr Sri Thakur stayed outside, Rabindranath visited Calcutta from Santiniketan. Rabindranath became disheartened and told Dr Dasgupta 'Doctor, looks like in this lifetime, I won't be able to meet your Gurudev. If there are articles written about him, or if there is a book written about his life's incidents, I would like to read that. By that, I will be able to remedy my pain somewhat, for not being able to meet him.' Listening to this, Dr Dasgupta gave some published papers documenting Ramthakur's life story and his miraculous deeds. Rabindranath was pleased after reading those documents. Then he said to Dr Dasgupta 'I felt quite happy after reading about your Gurudev's ascetic journey and his unbelievable acts. One has to be lucky enough to meet a person of that high saintly character and come in close contact. It is not happening with me in this lifetime. I heard one is born again if some desire remains unfulfilled. I am a believer in rebirth. So, I will spend the rest of my life with the belief that in my next birth my desire will be fulfilled. You have kept company with many sadhus. Do you know anyone who has achieved the perfection of spirituality? If you know, please arrange a visit for me. I am at present very much in mental distress.'

Dr Dasgupta understood the inner meaning of Rabindranath's words. He was not only the family physician but also a well-wisher. Rabindranath used to share his domestic woes with him and used to seek his advice. Dr Dasgupta never disappointed him. He always gave him the best advice.

Sometime back, Dasgupta had been introduced to *Yogiraj* Aghoribaba—an enlightened sadhu. Aghoribaba was born in 1845 at Pakur in Bihar. He was the maharajkumar of Pakur. In his youth, he came into contact with Bamakhyapa and very soon he was initiated by Bamakhyapa. Thereafter he travelled in the inaccessible snows of the Nepali Himalayas and subjected himself to severe ascetic practices. He achieved the highest level in both Yoga and Tantra sadhana at the same time. Within a short period, he was felicitated as the head of the Indian Nath community by the sadhus. He travelled, on foot, from the Himalayas to Kanyakumari and Assam to Dwarka three times. He meditated inside a snow covered cave at Mansarovar, Kailash for a long time and ultimately achieved his goal.

After some time, Aghoribaba reached Calcutta via Joydeb's fair. He met Dr Dasgupta at that time. Fortunately, Rabindranath was staying at Jorasanko Thakurbari then. Dr Dasgupta made the meeting between the two possible. Aghoribaba was residing at one of his disciple's homes, in north Calcutta. Rabindranath discussed with him about the Vaishnav creed, yoga, tantra and *Shaiva* sadhana for a good length of time. He felt happy about that. Rabindranath asked Aghoribaba if he would demonstrate some *Yogic Kriya* and superhuman power. Yogiraj Aghoribaba within a few seconds gave a demonstration. Rabindranath was stunned by this. He acknowledged his deepest gratefulness to Aghoribaba for this. He also thanked Dr Dasgupta.

Due to domestic problems, Rabindranath was mentally distraught at that time. In order to meet the financial demands made by his son Rathindranath and the unnecessary whims of his sons in law, he ran into financial debt. Not just once, but many times. Rabindranath's blessed *barobauma* (Hemlata Tagore— nephew Dwipendranath's wife) requested Rabindranath to give a little more money to Rathindranath because of his needs. Rabindranath was sad to hear this. He expressed his pain about this in a letter to Hemlata Tagore.

This letter is a memorable testimony of Nobel Prize winner

Rabindranath's simple lifestyle. Under what financial constraints he spent his life—this letter is invaluable proof of that!

Below is the letter he wrote to Hemlata:

'Dear Bauma, (daughter -in-law)

Your understanding that money is very necessary for people like Rathi, is only a blind superstition. If that statement was true, then only rich families would bring up real human beings and not the poor families. Your thinking that I am now sitting peacefully after having fulfilled all my financial needs is not correct. I have never enjoyed any pleasures bought with money—with God's blessing, most of the time in my life, I didn't have money at hand. Whatever little I had, I didn't use it for myself. I went through financial constraints like poor people – my biggest hobby was buying books, but I never had enough money to fulfill that wish. If today I long for money, then what I will pay to Rathi will infect him with the desire for worldly things.

If inside the son, the father grows to be more perfect— then you are fortunate. If Rathi turns out to be worldly, his lot will be bad—worse than mine.'

Receiving this letter from Rabindranath, Hemlata was stunned. She realised the mental agony of her highly respected *Kakamoshai.* She felt pain and remorseful for her letter. Later when she met Rabindranath, she sincerely apologised for unknowingly inflicting pain on the elderly Rabindranath. Ever forgiving, Rabindranath accepted affectionately her apology.

Rabindranath felt peace and happiness inside him after conversing with Aghoribaba. Yogiraj Aghoribaba talked about Bamakhyapa. Rabindranath happily told him about his and Mukunda Das's visit with Bamakhyapa. Rabindranath said 'I first heard about Bamakhyapa from my father (*babamoshai* –the Maharshi Debendranath Tagore). On Bamakhyapa's instruction and blessing, Bolpur Brahmacharya ashram was established. I heard a lot about him from Ramananda Bharati, Yogacharya Bhupendra Sanyal, and others. You are very lucky that you had the good fortune of having him as your Guru.'

After few hours of conversation, both Rabindranath and Dr Dasgupta returned happy and serene upon meeting Aghoribaba. This pleasant memory remained etched in their hearts. Aghoribaba lived a long life. He passed away while in deep meditation in Calcutta on 6 January 1980.

He was 135 years old when he left his mortal body. Netaji Subhas Chandra Bose was blessed by him, and enjoyed his divine company for quite some time.

Later on, though Rabindranath never again met Aghoribaba, Dr Dasgupta did meet him few more times.

RISHI AUROBINDO

YEAR 1905. The revolutionary period in Bengal was launched against the proposed partition of Bengal. The whole nation was in uproar against the partition. The whole of Bengal was mobilised against British barbarism and torture. 44 year-old Rabindranath joined the movement on the streets. As a symbol of Hindu Muslim unity, he tied coloured threads (Rakhi) on the wrists of people of both communities. People sang the song he had written on the occasion:

> *The soil of Bengal, The water of Bengal*
> *The air of Bengal, The produce of Bengal-*
> *May be blessed, may be blessed,*
> *May be blessed, O' my Lord.*

Henceforth, protests were incomplete without the singing of this song and the wearing of Rakhi. On the other side, an armed revolution started. The leader of that revolution was Arabinda Ghosh, associate editor of the *Bandemataram*, revolutionary and a believer in armed struggle.

Sister Nivedita brought Arabinda Ghosh to Bengal so that he could lead the armed movement in order to drive the British out of India for good. Arabinda translated Bankim Chatterji's book *Anandamath* into English. The history of the next chapter is known to all. Incidents relating to Arabinda's sentencing to

RISHI AUROBINDO

When the mind is still, then
Truth gets her chance to be
heard in the purity of the silence

jail with other revolutionaries, trial and finally release from jail are all documented in the history books.

At that time (24 August 1907), Rabindranath wrote to Arabinda saying, 'Arabinda, accept the salute from Rabindra.' Though Rabindranath was not a believer in violent revolution, he offered his sincere respect to Arabinda for his sacrifice.

The next chapter of Arabinda's life in the context of India's independence struggle, has remained memorable in India's history. Revolutionary Arabinda transformed himself to 'Rishi (the sage) Aurobindo'.

While spending time in jail, Arabinda's spiritual journey started that resulted in some miraculous developments including a visit from Lord Sri Krishna, the attainment of Raja Yoga sadhana by the disembodied soul of Swami Vivekananda, through the help of sister Nivedita, his shifting to Pondicherry from Chandennagore, completing Yoga sadhana under Raj Yogi 'Lele', and finally his attainment of enlightenment in Indian spirituality. Arabinda's life's documented version is contained in the book *Life Divine*, which has remained a priceless gift to India's spiritual world.

During this time, Rabindranath's winning of the Nobel Prize, becoming famous all over the world and receiving honours, travelling many times around the world added a memorable dimension to the world of literature.

Rishi Aurobindo is known in India and abroad as a Mahayogi, a person of wisdom and a great poet. His book *Savitri* is recognised as one of the greatest literary works of modern times by educationists. Aurobindo, therefore, is termed as the 'Official Male' in India's spiritual life.

On the other hand, Rishi poet Rabindranath, was a spiritualist, great poet, philosopher, literary writer, song writer, musician, and the world's most multi-talented individual. In short, he was the spokesperson of India's soul. A small incident on this subject is mentionable.

The word 'Yogi' means someone whose mind is directed towards God. His mind's desires remain insulated. He neither becomes overwhelmed with joy nor does he become depressed in times of sorrow. That person is recognised as a yogi and wise. By Yoga Sastra, it means that person has reached *porabastha* (next stage or final stage). That means that person has attained perfection in his/her sadhana. In terms of the Vedanta it is reaching brahmistithi (Godhead).

In the year 1913, Rabindranath was wandering around Santiniketan with his assistant Nepal Roy and was discussing how to fix the drainage system and maintain hygienic condition in the compound. Right at that time, a telegram reached him from the Swedish Academy in Stockholm. It informed him that for literature, he was awarded the Nobel Prize.

The highest award at that time carried a monetary gift of one lakh rupees (in today's value more than crores). Rabindranath quietly opened the telegram, read it, and then handed it over to Nepal Roy. He then said, 'Finally, there will be a way out in solving the drainage system and keep the compound hygienic.'

Nepal babu and others present there, thought somebody must have sent money for building the drains upon Rabindranath's request. But after reading the telegram, Nepal Roy was dumb struck. It was unfathomable to Nepal Roy how unattached Rabindranath was about the rare honour he had received in the form of a literary award and the amount of its monetary value. Rabindranath was least concerned about his personal glory. His interest was in how to improve his educational institution.

Within moments, through Nepal Roy, this happy news was announced in Santiniketan. The entire campus burst into a festive mood. But Rabindranath remained quiet as usual. This evidence of self-control, complete non-attachment to worldly honours, has not happened again in the history of the Nobel Prize.

Nobel Prize winners have usually reacted by becoming overjoyed, restless, speechless in surprise, while their colleagues and associates went around spreading the good news gleefully to all and sundry. Rabindranath was an exception. He who has practiced non-attachment and has therefore been able to unite his soul with the supreme spirit – that person can exert such type of self-control regardless of the circumstances. Rabindranath therefore was a great yogi – a true seer. This sage poet Rabindranath came to Rishi Aurobindo's ashram at Pondicherry in 1928. His objective was to visit the 'Official Male' of India's spiritual world. At that time, Rabindranath's generous mind was immersed in deep spirituality. This can be understood from the unforgettable song he had written a little while ago – the song reflects the sweet beauty of his deep spiritual consciousness. The song goes like this:

> *My heart sings at the wonder of my place*
> *In this world of light and life;*
> *At the feel in my pulse of the rhythm of creation*

Cadenced by the swing of the endless time.
I feel the tenderness of the grass in my forest walk,
The wayside flowers startle me:
That the gifts of the infinite are strewn in the dust
Wakens my song in wonder.
I have seen, have heard, have lived;
In the depth of the known have felt
The truth that exceeds all knowledge
Which fills my heart with wonder, and I sing.

(The above translation was by Rabindranath Tagore himself)

Rabindranath was pleased beyond measure after meeting Sri Aurobindo and enjoying an uplifting divine discussion. The 67-year-old poet took leave of him and returned home. After returning, he wrote, 'I did not have much time to talk to him. Within the little time I spent with him, I realised he is a powerhouse of easy inspiration. What a soothing glow in his tranquil and beautiful face!'

'I felt within you the word my father used to utter – you have become still by acquiring the supreme spirit. You are now connected to everyone, and you have entered inside them. That is the ultimate achievement of humanity according to Indian spirituality. Shakuntala's inauguration in the first hermitage happened out of youthful exuberance. The flourishing happened in the second hermitage when the soul became restful.'

'Today I saw him on the second ascetic seat – in speechless
silence.'
'Today I also told him by murmuring within myself
-Arabinda, accept my respect.'

BAUL NABANIDAS

BIRBHUM'S FAMOUS mystic folk singer Khyapa Baul Nabanidas came to Santiniketan at the invitation of world poet Rabindranath. At the appropriate time, this singer devoted to folk music and detached from worldly possessions, presented his exquisite written songs to Rabindranath who was mesmerised by these folk songs wrapped in deep spirituality. He became very respectful towards this saintly singer. At the end of his singing, Rabindranath asked Nabanidas, 'You are the descendant of the Gosain family. By family tradition, you are immersed in folk music and songs. I used to know your father – Akrur Gosain, an expert folk devotee. In Birbhum, he was recognised both as a folk devotee and an artist. But why did you give up your Gosain title for Khyapa?'

The mystic artist Nabanidas replied gently, 'You know my home is in Mallarpur. Near my house is situated the ancient tantrapith of Tarapith. I was initiated by Mahayogi Bamakhyapa of Tarapith.'

'I am blessed by his kindness and fortunate to have witnessed his Yoga miracles for a long time. He was the undivided being of the universal Tara Ma. In my path of devotion to music, his divine mercy is my strength. Not just from Birbhum, many devout and distinguished saints from Kashi, Vrindavan, Haridwar, Nilachal, etc. used to come to Tarapith to visit him. I

KHYAPA BAUL NABANIDAS

saw many of them. With Bamakhyapa's blessing, I wrote many songs and sang them before Sr Sri Tara Ma and Bamakhyapa.'

'On the auspicious day after the new moon, and with blessings from my Guru, I sang many times in front of devotees. As a token of respect to my Guru, I use the portion of my Guru's name as my first name. Many of his disciples have adopted the title *khyapa*. For example, enlightened Mahatma Tarakhyapa, Jagatkhyapa, Purnokhyapa, Manohorkhyapa, Manmohonkhyapa and others.'

Rabindranath kept quiet after hearing this. Then very respectfully he said 'Yes, I have known about Sri Sri Bamakhyapa since long. I also heard from Ramananda Bharati, and Yogacharya Bhupendranath Sanyal. They went to Tarapith and received his blessing. Above all, my babamoshai (Maharshi Debendranath Tagore) told me a lot about him. I have heard he was instrumental in the establishment of the ashram at Bolpur. Babamoshai remained his admirer for his entire life. I heard from babamoshai that his Yogi Guru Mahayogi Bahera Baba went to Tarapith and met Bamakhyapa. I also went with Mukunda Das to meet him and received his blessing. We both witnessed his miraculous Yogic power and were amazed.'

At Rabindranath's request, Nabanidas happily spent some days at Santiniketan. This folk singer sang in complete indifference to material circumstances, accompanying himself with a one-stringed musical instrument—a divine expression could be noticed. Looking at this pious image, Rabindranath and other music lovers were deeply moved.

One day Nabanidas started singing one of his own songs.

The song goes like this:

You enchanted the world with Harinam
My lonely Nitai
If my Nitai calls out as Nitai Gaur
If he thinks he is Nitai
Gaur Dili can give alone Nitai
My Nitai is himself Gaur
Call him as Nitai Gaur
Nitai alone is wish-yielding tree
Giver of love, master of the universe
My Nitai has New look
Call out as Nitai Gaur
Universally present as man or woman
But as Nitai, alone Nitai.

Listening to this exquisite song, Rabindranath was extremely impressed. He asked the writer, song composer and singer Nabanidas to sing again. Nabanidas sang again in his beautiful mellifluous voice. Rabindranath enjoyed the lyrics to his heart's content. The song's language, tune and expression influenced Rabindranath so much that he wrote the following song:

If nobody listens to your call
Then go it alone, go it alone!
Oh, hey tragic traveller!
If nobody talks to you,
If everybody turns away from you
If everybody is afraid (of the truth)

Then open up your heart,
Speak alone (about) what's in your mind,
Oh, hey tragic traveller!
If everybody turns away
If nobody notices you -
While traversing the hard path
Then alone you tread under your bloodied feet.
All those spikes on the road.
Oh, hey tragic traveller!
If there is no light in sight
If the doors are shut by the dark & stormy night
Then let the claps of thunder set your heart ablaze.
And let it burn - alone
Dark and stormy night.

With time, this song became famous among the people of India. Especially, during Gandhiji's march from Ahmedabad to the Dandi coast, people were chanting this song.

Another song of Nabanidas attracted Rabindranath quite a bit. Nabanidas was singing totally immersed in his own mood. The song goes like this:

What kind of madman he is
Creating ruckus
Come and see this in the middle of the river
He is dancing and chanting Hari Hari
He is bald headed wearing torn stitched cloth
He doesn't respond
Only tears stream down his eyes

What kind of madman he is
Creating ruckus in the middle of the river
He is of fair complexion
Women get attracted
He has sandal - paste mark on his forehead
And so young in age
This madman says not to waste time
This earthly play is going to be over
Your embellishment is on its way out
After this no more journey
What kind of madman he is
Creating ruckus.

Rabindranath wrote a song later, following his love for this above song. He wrote:

Here is a funny lunatic,
Creating ruckus in the middle of the river
You all see.
I will follow him to be enchanted.
Will see the offshoot of love.

This song became quite popular with fun loving listeners who liked the folk mood and the tune.

One day Rabindranath asked Nabanidas about the significance of the folk mood, and the theory of folk music. Saint Nabanidas said 'Folk music is equivalent to having a relationship with your inner self. It is realising the universal spirit within your soul. It is the worshipping of the self-illuminating great God inside you. Only then he will be the man in your heart. Love is the basis for the pursuit of folk music. Through love and complete surrender, you will find the kind man in your heart.'

'Sri Sri Chaitanya is the idol symbolising spiritual consciousness born out of love and devotion. He spread the message of love and devotion across the nation. Sri Chaitanya manifested his action through two assistants - Adwaityo Mahaprabhu and Nityananda Mahaprabhu.'

'When Sri Sri Chaitanya Mahaprabhu was spreading his message of love and devotion from Nilachal to entire Bharat, then Adwaityo Mahaprabhu said 'Today the Chaitanya who is coming close to us, in order to recognise him, we will have to awaken our consciousness inside.'

Aul is saying
Listen, my friend Baul
I am not in the market to sell rice.

Therefore, during Kaliyuga, to attain consciousness, the mind needs to be insulated from the outside world. The tongue must carry pleasant words. Sweet spiritual words need to be spread far and wide by means of pleasant tunes. Only then will the inner awakening happen—and you will be able to find the loving man in your heart. As you enter deep inside yourself, you will meet the gem of consciousness. Your soul will disappear into the supreme spirit inside the temple of your body. Body temple is the happy abode for the *Param Brahma*.'

'Our aim, as folk singers, is to move around our body with

mental pleasure. And with a one-stringed instrument in your hand, you sing with proper tune and knowledge. Because the song itself is knowledge abandoned. The folk singer's primary objective is to feel knowledge both inside your soul and in the universe. That is why in folk songs, you not only have magical tunes but deep spiritual wisdom. The singer therefore says:

In every stanza there is material
Only if you understand.

'There is a common saying about folk songs—proper tune makes good music, music induces meditation, meditation leads to final release. You are complete when the final release of soul occurs. Therefore, the mood, devotion, music etc, of a folk singer are directed towards reaching this completeness. You realise the universe inside your body temple.'

Rabindranath felt quite happy after listening to Nabanidas's description of folk singing.

Gladly he said, 'I know you are the descendants of Gosain family aka Nityananda Mahaprabhu. I know your family tradition of folk singers for generations.'

Nabanidas was pleased to hear this and said, 'Your statement is correct. From Nityananda Prabhu till today, many great men were born in our family. Of them, Birbhadra, worthwhile son of Nityananda Mahaprabhu, must be mentioned. He was mainly a traveller. He wrote many songs. His songs carry so much wisdom. After him, Mahatma Rasaraj Gosain, Anant Gosain and Atul Gosain followed the tradition. They also wrote many folk songs. Through simple words and deep thinking, these songs have influenced endlessly the world of folk *sadhana*.

Atul Gosain was not only an enlightened person but also could travel in different bodies at the same time for the spiritual benefit of his disciples. He excelled in the practice of Hatha yoga. He predicted the time of his death several days in advance. He went into his final deep meditative state at the appointed hour. He was 110 years old when he left his mortal body.'

Nabanidas sang many more songs at the request of Rabindranath. These songs were written by Lalon Fakir, Gagan Harkara, Sirajsnai and other saints of Bengal. Nabanidas sang the following beautiful song written by Lalon Fakir:

> *I have seen in the sea of beauty*
> *The one of my hearts and most pure*
> *I keep thinking of catching him*
> *Went to catch him but I couldn't find him.*

Rabindranath, influenced by this song wrote:

> *Someone is driving me crazy from one pillar to the other.*
> *I want to know who that fanatic is.*
> *Nabanidas sang another song:*
> *"O' lord Bishnu, why is my golden Gaur here crying*
> *All the others are gone for chanting*
> *But why is my Gaur's body dusty*
> *What thought evoked him to roll over*
> *All the others are gone for chanting*
> *What thought evoked him to roll over in the courtyard*
> *All the others are chanting Hari Hari*

Some are clapping
Saying Radhe Radhe with tearful eyes
I fail to understand what is in your mind and in his mind.

Rabindranath captured the tune of the song and wrote the following immortal song:

O my native soil, I bow my head to you in deep obeisance.
In you rests the universe, on you is spread the love of the universal mother.

Rabindranath spent a wonderful time with folk singer Nabanidas for some days at Santiniketan. He conferred the title 'Khyapa' on him.

After this, Nabanidas visited Santiniketan from time to time, on invitation from Rabindranath, during which he would sing folk songs and discuss spiritual subjects.

Nabanidas expressed a desire to build a small coaching center for folk singing in the lap of Santiniketan's natural splendour. Rabindranath fulfilled this noble desire of Nabanidas. He offered Nabanidas land for this purpose at Bhubandanga. Rabindranath also liked the idea that Khyapa Nabanidas would be available all the time at the campus, and he would greatly enjoy Nabanidas's company.

Nabanidas built the desired coaching center at Bhubondanga. Both of them maintained a pleasant relationship till the end.

BUDDHA BOSE

RABINDRANATH MET Buddha Bose, internationally famous *Kriyayogi*, through Bhupendranath Sanyal. Buddha Bose was the worthy disciple of Yogi and body builder Bishnucharan Ghosh – youngest brother of America resident *Kriyayogi* Swami Yogananda.

Yogiraj Shyama Charan Lahiri's worthy disciple Bhupendranath Sanyal was appointed the Principal of Brahmacharya School at Santiniketan, at the request of Rabindranath. He carried out this duty with complete devotion for seven years. He was forced to take leave from Santiniketan due to ill health, but he maintained a pleasant relationship with Rabindranath till the end.

During the twilight of his life, Rabindranath felt a special attraction towards the practices of the *Kriya* yoga, a discipline founded by Yogiraj Shyamacharan Lahiri Mahasay. Before this, Rabindranath had met, in Kashi, the elderly Yogi Krishnaramji who informed Rabindranath about the secrets of *Kriya* yoga. Krishnaramji who was the religious preceptor of Bhupendranath Sanyal - worthy disciple of Shyamacharan Lahiri Mahasay.

When Bhupendranath was the principal of the Brhamhacharya school at Santiniketan, he apprised Rabindranath about *Kriya* yoga. Rabindranath developed an abiding respect for Lahiri Mahasay Gurudev of Bhupendra

BUDDHA BOSE

Sanyal. But due to his many responsibilities—going abroad, writing books, giving lectures around the world, running the administration of Visvabharati—Rabindranath couldn't focus single mindedly on learning *Kriya* yoga. However, he had the deep desire to learn this great yoga sadhana. By regularly practicing this spiritual exercise, he earnestly wanted to keep his body and mind fit and fresh.

Now in the twilight of his life, he found some break from his activities, to learn *Kriya* yoga. He was 78 years old then. He enquired extensively about this subject from Bhupendranath Sanyal. Both Bhupendranath and *Kriyayogi* Buddha Bose were at Santiniketan upon an invitation by Rabindranath.

Bhupendranath explained the impact of *Kriya* yoga on day-to-day life and spirituality. Even after shouldering family responsibilities, performing *Kriya* yoga, in the early morning and just before sunset, helps the human body to remain disease-free and enjoy a long happy life. This is the external benefit of *Kriya* yoga. But the internal benefit is far reaching. *Kriya* yoga taught the practitioner proper sitting posture for meditation, breathing exercises etc, which help the ascetic person to internalise inner energy to a still position and finally attain the personified energy of Brahma.

Kriya yoga practitioner meets the God worshipped, through visionary wisdom, connects humanity with its inner soul and reaches an extraordinarily blissful state of mind. He also gains miraculous powers out of yoga. In a moment the yogi can leave his gross physical body, and with the help of the subtle body reach, hear, see, and understand anything in any part of the universe, and use that energy for beneficial purpose. In the sacred book of Gita, Sri Krishna spoke to Arjuna about *Kriya* yoga. Rabindranath was highly impressed after learning about Lahiri Mahasay's divine life.

Rabindranath realised that the ultimate aim of *Kriya* yoga was to elevate the human soul to a point where it is dissolved in the supreme power (*paramatma*). The wished for deity in *Kriya* yoga is the highest being, Sri Krishna. In every breath, the mantra is *Aum*. This *Aum* is the symbol of formless, unconditioned essence of the universe – Brahma. Rabindranath realised that through *Kriya* yoga not only could humans become free of worldly disease and ageing, they could also reach divinity while remaining in their flesh and blood bodies—the ultimate aim of life. In the Upanishads, the sages were repeatedly advising humans about reaching this personified energy of Brahma.

Therefore, Rabindranath informed Bhupendranath that he was prepared to learn *Kriya* yoga. He wanted to traverse both worldly and spiritual paths. He was 78 years then and was suffering from diseases due to age. He suffered from hemorrhoids for a long time and had surgery in England. He still suffered from this from time to time. In addition, he was at that time suffering quite a bit from complications of the prostate gland.

Above all, it was the gall bladder that made him suffer the most. So, to get rid of these diseases, he told Bhupendranath that he thought Lahiri Mahasay's *Kriya* yoga would help. However, Bhupendranath was hesitant about Rabindranath's taking up *Kriya* yoga due to his age and prevailing health conditions.

Kriya yoga needs to be started from a young age. When it is started at an age when the body is fit and strong, you can excel in that practice very rapidly and illness cannot touch you in your mature life. The *Kriya* yoga practitioner can live disease-free till he leaves his body at his will. Bhupendra Sanyal was initiated in *Kriya* yoga at the age of 16. Within two years by the age of 18, he had mastered the subject. Yogiraj Lahiri Mahasay had asked Bhupendra to give initiation to many people across India. This is quite rare. One can learn at middle age also provided one is bodily fit and strong. But Rabindranath at age 78 was suffering from disease and therefore he was not at all fit for learning *Kriya* yoga.

At that time, Rabindranath's mind was also searching for life's relationship with the infinite. It was as if Rabindranath's soul was trying to leave this disease- and grief- ridden body and mind for good. He, therefore, wrote at that age:

Ahead flows the river of peace.

Set sail O boatman.

You will be my constant companion, accept me into your fold —

The stars will light the path of infinity.

O Saviour, your grace, your mercy

Will be the fare for the eternal journey.

May the shackles of the world end; the vast universe spread

its arms,

And without fear, fathom within, the grand unknown.

However, due to the earnest request from Rabindranath, Bhupendranath agreed to unravel the intricacies of *Kriya* yoga. It was made clear that what Rabindranath was initiated with, will be his alone and could not be shared with anyone else. After this, Bhupendra asked the 31-year-old and world-famous yogi Buddha Bose to demonstrate the specific yogic postures and breathing techniques in front of Rabindranath. Buddha Bose had taught many people in England and America these practices of *Kriya* yoga. He had reached the pinnacle in this field of Yoga *sadhana*. His physical beauty and elegance were extraordinary. To Rabindranath, he appeared to be a handsome young man of only 19-20 years.

Buddha Bose's sculptured body and face were so tender and unblemished, that many considered him to be an adolescent.

Anyway, Rabindranath watched Buddha Bose's demonstrations for quite some time and learnt from it. Buddha Bose's explanation pleased Rabindranath.

By the way, Rabindranath had made a remark about 'ancient India's hermitage culture, where beautiful and pious children used to participate in religious activities with great success. Looking at Buddha Bose, I am reminded of one of those children'. Therefore, this teacher of Rabindranath was honoured by Rabindranath as 'the sage child'. He took a picture with Buddha Bose and presented him with a congratulatory write up.

Only ten months before this meeting, Buddha Bose had demonstrated this ancient yogic exercise to Jawaharlal Nehru in London and explained everything in English.

Nehru was a great admirer of India's Yoga Sadhana. He used to practice this every day. Nehru was very impressed with Buddha Bose's demonstration. Nehru learnt some additional yoga postures from Buddha Bose. One of Bose's gurus who also happened to be his father-in-law Sri Bishnu Charan Ghosh—yogacharya and body builder—was also there, and Mr Ghosh talked about the usefulness of Yoga to Nehru. Mr Bose and Mr Ghosh met Nehru in London on their way to America. Seeing the ancient glory of India's yoga being spread in the western world by these two gentlemen, Nehru was so pleased that he wrote a congratulatory note to them and wished them great success.

Rabindranath had met Bishnu Charan Ghosh before too. Mr Ghosh took his brother Sananda Ghosh to Santiniketan to meet Rabindranath. Many people may not know the universally famous picture of Rabindranath (wearing the gown, with hands behind and little stooped) was snapped by Bishnu Charan Ghosh. But in order to make his brother Sananda Ghosh popular he named his brother as the photographer and had that endorsed by Rabindranath.

Buddha Bose's life story of meeting with accident and getting miraculously saved, recovering from serious illness at Kedarnath, trekking on foot thirteen times to Mansarovar and Kailash are written in the history books. His life is full of God's blessing and miraculous events. He had written two timeless books, viz. *Holy Kailash* and *Key to the kingdom of health*.

His brief life story is as follows. Buddha Bose was born on 10 August 1908. His father Raja Bose was a famous magician. Buddha Bose's mother was a British woman. Buddha Bose was very handsome. In his adolescent years, he was treated affectionately by Yogiraj Lahiri Mahasay and *Kriyayogi* Bhagabati Charan Ghosh. Bose was initiated into *Kriya* yoga by his father-in-law's elder brother, the America resident Swami Yogananda, but the inner meaning of *Kriya* yoga was taught to him by Bhagabati Charan Ghosh, father of Swami Yogananda. And the emotional *sadhana* and *Yogasanas* were taught to him by his father-in-law Bishnu Charan Ghosh. With the help of these three enlightened yogis, Bose made advancements in his *Kriya* yoga *sadhana*. He added, to these teachings, the God given power that he inherited from his previous births.

At the age of 21 (year 1929), he travelled on foot to the Manasarovar Lake and Mount Kailash. Inaccessible Tibet was banned for travel to the entire world. He, however, showing enormous courage and undergoing extreme pain, entered Tibet. He travelled to Tibet twice after that. At this time, he met a Mahayogi at the Mount Kailash at a height of 19000 feet. That Mahayogi told him, 'Though you are very much inclined to meditate here at Mansarovar and Kailash, you are destined to do altogether different activities. You will have to continue your *sadhana* by staying with your family. You will have to marry. You will have two sons. Later you will have a daughter. You will be visiting abroad many times for your work. You will face an airline accident. Boarding the plane, you will notice the seat next to you is vacant. Just before the accident happens, you will see me sitting in that seat. Many people will die in that accident, but with the blessing of Krishna, you will survive. But a part of your body will be broken and burnt. After that with the blessing of Shiva, you will completely recover.' After that, the enlightened Yogi told Bose exactly when that accident would happen.

After hearing this from the kind *mahapurush*, Bose, a depressed person, returned to his Calcutta home.

After some time, Bose was married to Yogacharya Bishnu Charan Ghosh's daughter. This marriage was basically administered by Bishnu Charan's father Bhagabati Charan Ghosh. Bhagabati Charan had planned this marriage much earlier. Bose started his married life. Side by side Bose continued his Yoga *sadhana*. In his work life, he continued doing export and import business with England and America. He became the father of two sons. Finally, the time came near for the plane accident as forecast by that *mahapurush*. Buddha Bose had to visit America due to business reasons. When all the previous forecasts as determined by the Kailash sadhu did happen, this one too was going to happen. Anticipating this danger, all relatives and in laws asked Bose not to take this trip to America. However, his religious and spirited wife, with complete faith in God, gave permission for the trip of her husband.

At the right time, the airline ticket was purchased. But just before the plane was to take off at the appointed time, some technical problems cropped up. Hearing this, Buddha Bose went to the airlines company and wanted the ticket to be returned. During his conversation, he mentioned his meeting with the sadhu in Tibet and informed them that all his predictions so far had materialised. He was certain this plane accident prediction would also happen. Therefore, he wasn't travelling by that plane. He wanted to return his ticket. One of the pilots, an Anglo-Indian, listened to what Bose said. Then he said, 'Okay Mr. Bose, I accept the plane will meet with an accident. But did that Sadhu tell you that you would die in this accident?' Bose said, 'No'. The pilot then said, 'Then why wouldn't you go? Besides that, do you think all the 42 passengers that are travelling are destined to die? That may not happen.' Listening to this, Bose desisted from cancelling the ticket and decided to go to America.

At the appointed time, Bose boarded the plane and saw as per prediction, the seat next to him was vacant.

The plane took off at the right time. When the plane was crossing over the middle east countries, suddenly some technical problem surfaced. One of the wings caught fire. Losing control, the plane dropped. Momentarily, the plane burst into flames. Suddenly, Bose saw that Tibet *mahapurush* was sitting in the chair next to him. The sadhu reassured him and vanished. Immediately, the flames engulfed Bose. He drew his two legs onto his chair. His body was burning. He bitterly cried out to his tutelary deity Krishna. 'God, I can't bear this pain anymore. Give me death. Take me to your lap.' The inside of the aircraft was on fire. Terrible fire, choking smoke, and horrid screaming filled the airplane. The burning aircraft dropped at terrific speed, crashed to the ground, and broke into pieces. The wreckage of the plane, dead bodies and half burnt almost dead bodies were scattered over an area of a few square miles.

Buddha Bose was also heavily burnt, and he was flung on to the hard ground. His spinal cord was broken to pieces, and he became unconscious. After quite some time, the rescue team came, lifted Bose and some badly burnt almost dying people and admitted them to a nearby hospital. After recovering a little bit, Bose went to America for treatment. After receiving the most advanced treatment, Bose could barely walk around wearing a steel jacket. After some more time, he developed some side effects in his body. Doctors suspected it to be bone TB. There was a need for a replacement of the lumbar. It was decided the operation would take place in America. The foreign doctor who was to do the operation, had been fortunately, initiated into *Kriya* yoga by Buddha Bose. Bose disclosed everything about the meeting with the sadhu in Tibet to this doctor. Hearing everything, the doctor said to his *Kriya* yoga Guru, 'If you go to Tibet again, that sadhu with divine power if he wants to cure you, will be able to do it perfectly. But if I operate on you with an artificial lumbar, it may not be perfect like the original. You decide what you will do.'

Hearing this, Bose decided not to do the operation. He came to India from America. He was as usual wearing the steel jacket.

After a while, Buddha Bose, along with a coworker, started out on his pilgrimage to Kedarnath, Badrinath, Gangotri, Jamunotri, and Gomukh. Despite his disabled body, he set out on foot. Finally, he reached snow covered sacred Kedarnath at an altitude of 11750 feet. The triangular shaped Kedarnath's Shiva lingam is one of the very potent and the best among the dozen *jyotirlingams*. Bose started his chanting with proper breathing in front of this *jyotirlingam* dating from the war described in the epic poem *Mahabharata*. One had to be very lucky to be able to perform *Kriya* yoga in front of Yogeswar Mahadev.

Suddenly, in a meditative state, Bose saw, standing before him, the glowing white king of Gods, Mahadev. Mahadev asked Bose to chant a particular sacred word one lakh times and that would cure him of all ailments. When Bose opened his eyes after receiving this word, he found that the Shiva image had vanished. Instead, a white glowing pillar was stationed in front of him. After a while, that faded away too.

It was midnight then. He started chanting. After he chanted 5000 times, Kedarnath reappeared and told him the chanting wasn't being done correctly. He showed the proper way to chant and then vanished. Bose saw the time in the watch was 4.00 am. That meant the sacred moment just before dawn had started. At this holy moment, Bose started his chanting from the beginning. He continued chanting the whole day and night. Next day by 6 am, he had completed one lakh chants while sitting in the same position and then he offered respectful pranam to Kedarnath before getting up.

To his utter surprise, Buddha Bose observed he was absolutely fit and his spine normal and strong.

With unbounded happiness, he took off the steel jacket and threw it into the flowing sacred Mandakini water. His coworker tried to stop him from doing that by saying 'You made a big mistake. You would need that steel jacket again.'

Hearing this, the ascetic Bose, who had been blessed by the lord of Kedarnath, said with extreme confidence, 'In this life I will never need that jacket again.'

And so it happened. He didn't need that jacket ever again. He lived the rest of his life happily, without any ailment.

After that, he visited Badrinarayan, Gangotri, Jamunotri, and Gomukh. After some time, he set out again on foot, visiting for the fourth time, Kailash, and Manasarovar.

The divine scenario of Kailash and Manasarovar had beckoned him over and over again.

Altogether he visited that place 13 times. No other yogi traveller like Bose had visited Kailash-Mansarovar so many times,

During these travels, Bose realised that crores of Indians could not visit the sacred places due to lack of good health and conducive climate. Therefore, he decided to capture the images of these places on a camera and then show it to the people of India. Accordingly, he took pictures (in colour and black and white) of great pilgrimage centres, temples and even symbols of sacred stones. Surprisingly, nowhere was he obstructed from taking pictures.

This great work of Buddha Bose was appreciated throughout India. He started giving initiation in *Kriya* yoga to multitudes of deserving people both in India and abroad.

Later in life, he established his 'Yoga Cure Center' at New Alipore, Calcutta and cured many people from grave ailments.

The Mahapurush from Tibet had taught a special *Kriya* yoga to Bose. With the help of that *Kriya*, a person suffering from grave illness and facing sure death, could be saved, and cured completely within a certain time. However, there was a condition behind it. The condition was, if Bose would cure that person with that special *Kriya*, Bose would not see that person ever again. If he did, he would die of that disease very soon.

Bose, by this *Kriya* had cured many people but never saw them again. One day, Bose's compassionate wife saw a dying relative of hers, and requested Bose to cure the relative. Bose quietly said, 'I can cure that person, but I will never see that person's face again.' Bose's wife said, 'How is that possible? Since that person is our relative, there is every possibility we would meet that person in social gatherings.' Listening to this Bose said with a grave voice, 'If you are willing to become a widow, take me to your relative. I will cure your relative.' After hearing this, Bose's wife didn't dare to take her husband to her relative.

In 1951 Bose was blessed with a daughter. He named her Ruma. With time she grew to be an appropriate daughter, befitting her illustrious father. Noticing her spiritual growth and as a deserving candidate for teaching *Kriya* yoga, Bose initiated her. Side by side he made her an expert in *yogasanas*. Later in life, after her marriage, Ruma Devi established a yoga cure center at Kalighat, Calcutta, and dedicated her life to it. Ruma Devi, upon the divine intervention of Lahiri Mahasay, gave initiation in *Kriya* yoga to many pure and deserving people. She is still carrying on the spiritual tradition of her departed father.

On 27 April 1983, Buddha Bose, at the age of 75, left his mortal body while he was fully conscious under deep meditation. From the spiritual sky of India, a luminous star departed into infinity.

ENLIGHTENED MOTHER

THE HOLI festival we are about to speak of was held in March 1938. With full splendor, the spring festival was celebrated in Santiniketan. Centering around world poet Rabindranath, Santiniketan students, along with a huge number of admirers took part in the festivities.

During this occasion, while Rabindranath was peeling a cucumber in his room, Sri Sri Ranga Ma, a great ascetic from Tarapith, Birbhum, entered Rabindranath's room. Ranga Ma was accompanied by Samar Sen, her devotee. The 77-year-old sage poet Rabindranath, surprised at seeing this spiritual looking lady, respectfully asked, 'Where are you coming from, Mother? What do you want?' Hearing this, the 44-year-old ever smiling mighty Ranga Ma said, 'I am coming from Tarapith. I haven't come here to see how famous you are. I have come to see your quality.' Hearing this, Rabindranath smiled happily. Then laughingly answered her, 'But mothers never find fault with their children. They only notice their quality'. Ranga Ma smiled a little. After a while, Ranga Ma took leave of Rabindranath and returned to her ashram at Hazra Road, Calcutta.

Six months after this visit, in October 1938, at the end of the Sharodiya Durga Puja, and on the fourteenth day, Sri Sri Tara Puja as usual, was organised at Tarapith. The great ascetic

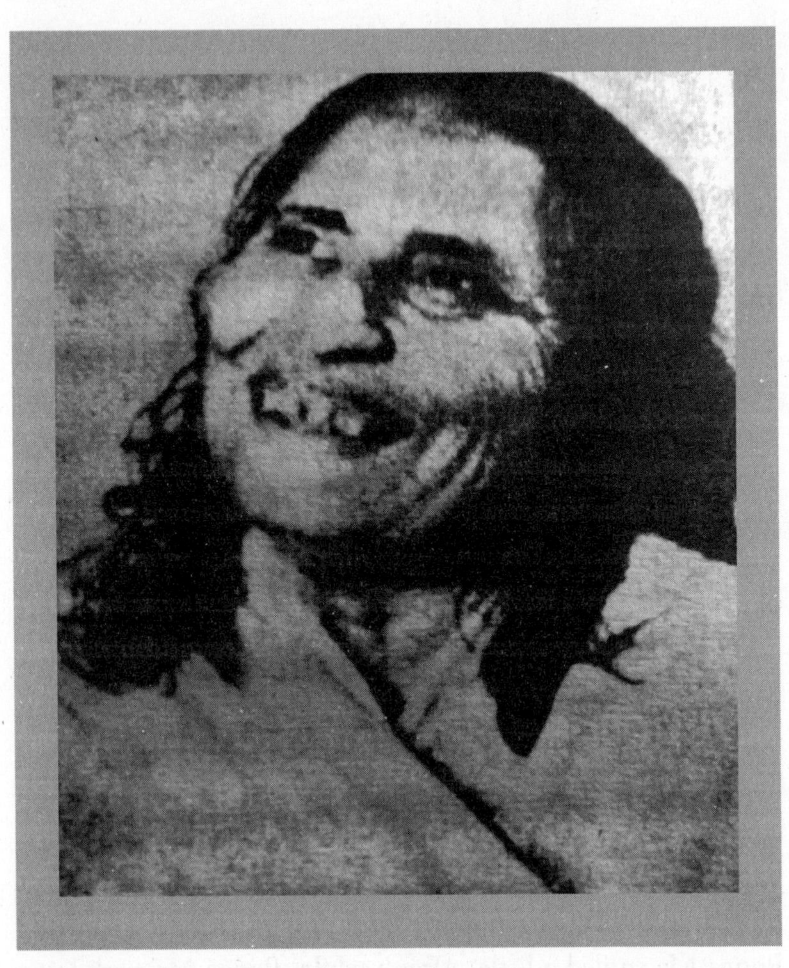

SRI SRI RANGA MA

Lady Ranga Ma came from Calcutta with her disciples to join in this great festive occasion. For seven days, the religious proceedings went on. On this occasion, a good deal of folk music was sung and a village fair was held for seven days. Nabanidas, a favourite disciple of Sri Sri Bamakhyapa, the life force at Tarapith, presented his songs and music in front of thousands of devotees.

In the past, Rabindranath, and folk singer Mukunda Das had visited Bamakhyapa and received his blessings. Besides them, Mahayogi Bahera Baba, Narendranath Dutta (later known Swami Vivekananda), Ramananda Bharati, Bhupendra Nath Sanyal and many other sadhus came to Tarapith and received blessings from Sri Sri Bamakhyapa. They all were well known to Rabindranath. Therefore, this ancient religious abode had a special place in Rabindranath's heart.

After attending the Puja at Tarapith, Ranga Ma again came with her disciples to visit Rabindranath at Santiniketan. This was the second visit in 6 months and as usual her disciple Samar Sen was also present.

Autumn had spread her quiet beauty all around Santiniketan. It was nearly 9 in the morning. Ranga Ma came to know that the poet was unwell. People were prohibited from meeting him at this time. However, Ranga Ma was deemed as the living image of Tara Ma of Tarapith. People had seen her performing miraculous deeds for so many people. Therefore, it was not possible to stop Ranga Ma from seeing Rabindranath. Ranga Ma entered Rabindranath's room accompanied by disciple son Samar Sen.

The poet was standing alone lost in himself. As there was no chair available for sitting, Rabindranath arranged for one. Sitting on the chair, Ranga Ma started talking—'I am the mother from Tarapith. I have come to see you, my son. I heard you were not doing well.'

The 78-year-old Rabindranath answered gently, 'Yes, I became sick. However, with your blessing, I am better now. You have come after quite a while.'

Rabindranath hadn't forgotten her previous visit six months ago. The person whose mind was always in search of pious minds, obviously didn't forget a great ascetic lady like Ranga Ma.

But at this old age, nearing eighty and being in ill health, it wasn't natural to remember her previous visit. More so, because in the last six months, the poet had had to write endlessly, work, travel, give lectures and meet hundreds of visitors. But there was no one to compare with Rabindranath. He was unique in his own rights. He was born on this earth with divine power and unparalleled memory.

After conversation on various topics, Ranga Ma stood up from the chair and very affectionately said 'Pray to God, my son. Everything will turn out good for you.' The poet just smiled but didn't say anything.

Rabindranath accompanied Ranga Ma to the door with due respect. Ranga Ma returned to her ashram in Calcutta.

Rabindranath started his first meeting with Ramkrishna as part of his quest to meet sadhus and ended with Ranga Ma. So, both the memories of two sacred places Dakhineswar and Tarapith remained etched in Rabindranath's mind.

Bhabatarini of Dakshineshwar and Tarini of Tarapith have blessed Jorasanko and Santiniketan respectively.

It is as if Rabindranath realised his soul's worshipper was the ever-lasting and ever-loving universal mother. That is why he sang:

Mother, just stand for a second,

Let me look at your beautiful face.

Where will you go abandoning us in dark,

In the vacant home.

Your sweet smiling face

Dripping nectar in abundance

If you leave with your smile

How are we going to nourish our soul.

Once, the poet wrote two great songs in the name of universal mother—'Cry out in the name of Kali' and 'My mother, my creator, I prostrate at your crimson lotus feet; Under this dense darkness, I worship Ma Tara.'

Ma Kali and Ma Tara protected the poet throughout his life with wisdom and bliss. Despite the flaming suffering distress, the poet had to endure, the goddess mother's never-ending affection kept him glowing with divine power. Having been blessed, Rabindranath wrote in the beginning of his youth:

Ma Kali, adorned with a chain of heads, where did you learn

all these tricks.

Seeing your dance, the mind trembles, the earth is shocked.

Give us a respite, please calm down – your son is begging,

O third eye holder powerful mother,

Let me close my eyelids watching your red shot eyes.

GLOSSARY

Adi:	First and superior
Advaita:	Advaita is a Sanskrit word that translates as 'not two' or 'no second'. This gives the idea that the inner Self, or *Atman*, is the same as the Absolute Reality, that is *Brahman*.
Amritam:	Nectar
Anandam:	Full of joy
Ashram:	Hermitage
Atma:	Often translated as soul but in Sanskrit it is the cosmic self
Babamoshai:	Revered father
Badrinath:	It is a Hindu holy place in Uttarakhand.
Balmiki Pratibha:	The genius of Valmiki is an opera by Rabindranath Tagore
Baroma:	Elder mother
Baul:	A member of a nonconformist Bengalis sect having gurus but no dogmas, rituals, religious institutions, or scriptures.
Bhabatarini:	Goddess Kali Ma - historically famous for Dakshineswar Kali Temple
Bharati sect:	One of the sects of Hindu religion
Brahma:	The ultimate ground of all being in Hinduism
Brahmachari:	Celibate

Brahmo:	It is monotheistic sect of Hinduism.
Chaitanya deb:	Chaitanya Mahaprabhu was a 15th century Indian saint.
Chandi:	It is the demon-destroying form of the Hindu goddess Durga.
Chatim tree:	Blackboard tree
Dadu Kabir:	The poet-mystic from Rajasthan, India
Dharma:	Divine law
Dhrupad:	It is the oldest surviving classical Hidustani vocal music
Duality:	Two aspects of something
Durga Devi:	Durga means invincible. Durga Devi represents Goddess Durga in Hinduism.
Gaur:	Fair-skinned
Gayatri Mantra:	A universal prayer on the glory of the Creator
Gita:	The Gita, believed to be the advice of Lord Krishna, is a 700-verse Hindu scripture that is part of the epic Mahabharata.
Gurubhai:	Fellow disciple of the same spiritual guide
Gyanganj:	The dwelling of immortals, is situated in an isolated valley in the Himalayas.
Hari Hari:	Lord Krishna is known as Hari. Chanting Hari Hari, it is believed, all the inauspicious things from the devotee are taken away.
Harinam:	The chanting of lord Krishna's holy name
Hatha Yoga:	The school of Yoga that stresses mastery of the body as a way of attaining a state of spiritual perfection in which the mind is withdrawn from external objects.

Jeevan Smriti:	Memoirs
Jorasanko:	It is a neighborhood of North Calcutta (Where the Tagore family residence is situated)
Jyotirlingam:	A devotional representation of the Hindu god Shiva
Kakamoshai:	respected uncle
Kaliyug:	The age of vice and misery
Kashi:	It is also called Varanasi, a holy city in Uttar Pradesh, India
Khyapa:	Eccentric
Kirtan:	It is the act of praising and glorifying some form of divinity.
Kriya Yogi:	A person who practices a number of levels of pranayama, mantra, and mudra, intended to rapidly accelerate spiritual development.
Mahabharata:	The other great epic of India, set down in writing in Sanskrit about 200 Bc.
Mahadev:	The great god is one of the principal deities of Hinduism.
Mahapith Tarapith:	It is a sacred place located in the Birbhum district of West Bengal, India.
Mahapurush:	Great being.
Maharshi:	A religious sage
Mahasadhika:	A great female student practicing meditation.
Mahasatipith:	One of the fifty-one great old sacred places of the Goddess Shakti

Mahatantrik:	Those who by practicing meditation have succeeded in weaving physical with the spiritual being.
Mahayogi:	Great among those who practice yoga
Mahayogi:	It is someone who has attained enlightenment.
Mandir:	Temple
Mantra *Shakti:*	It is the universal cosmic energy as personified by the Hindu mother goddess, Shakti, that is evoked by the repetitive recitation of a single syllable, word, or series of phrases.
Mirabai:	She was a 16th-century Hindu mystic poet and devotee of Krishna.
Nilachal:	The abode of Hindu deity Jagannath at Puri is known as the Nilachala
Param Brahma:	The supreme being, the source of all creation. According to Hinduism, Shiva, Vishnu, Brahma, and Shakti are all manifestations of Param Brahman.
Paramahansa:	A sannyasi of the highest level of spiritual development in which union with ultimate reality is attained.
Paramatma:	Supreme soul
Parampurush:	Supreme Personality
Patanjali:	Born 200 BC. He was an author, mystic, and philosopher. He compiled the yoga sutra.
Prasad:	Food and water offered to a deity during worship (puja) in India
Puranas:	It is any of 18 collections of Hindu legends and religious instructions.

Raktakarabi:	A red oleander of Indian origin
Ramayana:	It is one of the most compelling Indian epics written by the sage Valmiki.
Rishi:	A Hindu sage
Sadhak:	Seeker of truth
Sadhana:	Daily spiritual practice
Samaj:	society
Sankhya darshanas:	It is one of India's six philosophical schools (darshans).
Sarangi:	An Indian bowed musical instrument
Satipitha:	Sacred place of eternal power
Satsang:	The practice of gathering in the company of good people for the performance of devotional activities.
Sejobabu:	Sejo in Bengali means third brother out of four age wise.
Shaiva:	Relating to the God Shiva
Shakto:	Worshipper of strength
Shivalinga:	It represents Lord Shiva in Hinduism and embodies all the energy of the world and beyond.
Siddha Tantrik:	A tantrik who has attained perfection or supernatural abilities.
Siddha Yogi:	A yogi who has attained enlightenment with the help of meditation and breathing exercises.
Siddhi:	The spiritual gifts that activate upon enlightenment.
Slokas:	A Sanskrit verse of praise

Sufi:	A Muslim who represents the mystical dimension of Islam;
Swarodoy Yoga:	It is the yoga practice of the Vedic science that understands the function of the nasal cycle.
Tanpura:	An instrument of Indian music
Tantrapitha:	Sacred place where tantrik practices meditation.
Tantrik dristiyoga:	Yoga which is a focused gaze, as a means for developing concentrated intention.
Tantrik yoga:	The main difference between tantrik and historical yoga is that while tantric techniques and rituals primarily focus on the cultivation and build-up of kundalini energy, the regular yoga promotes endurance, strength, calmness, flexibility, and well-being.
Tantrism:	It focuses upon ritual aspects that involve the use of the physical in sacred and worshipful settings to access the supernatural.
Tarama:	Goddess Kali
Thakur:	Bengali version of Tagore
Transcedental:	Being beyond common or ordinary experience
Upanishad:	Each of a series of Hindu sacred treatises written in Sanskrit between 800 and 500 BCE
Vaishnav:	Worshipper of Lord Vishnu
Vedanta:	The earliest sacred literature of India. "Veda" means the Knowledge and "anta" means the end of it.
Vedas:	A large body of religious texts originating in ancient India

Yoga darshan:	Yoga darshana is one of the six darshanas, or ways of viewing the world, according to Hindu philosophy.
Yoga:	A Hindu spiritual and ascetic discipline
Yogacharya:	A title of respect given to a teacher of yoga
Yogi Baba:	Respected yogi
Yogi raj:	Great ascetic
Yogic:	A practice or action that creates a unification of the body, mind, soul, and universal consciousness.
Yogiraj:	It is a title of Shiva, meaning king of yoga

DATA REGISTER

Jibon (Jeevan) Smriti: Rabindranath Tagore

Chelebela: Rabindranath Tagore

Balmiki (Valmiki) Protiva: Rabindranath Tagore (musical play)

Gitanjali (Book of poetry): Rabindranath Tagore

Gitabitan (1st,2nd,3rd part): Rabindranath Tagore

Sanchayita: Rabindranath Tagore

Patrabali (letters) (1-16 part): Rabindranath Tagore

Gitabitan according to years: Prabhat Kumar Mukhopadhyay

Brahma Sangeet: Published by Brahmo Samaj

Smritikatha: Mahayogi Baherababa

Smritikatha: Yogiraj Ramnath Aghoribaba

Smritikatha: Dr Jatindra Mohon Dasgupta

Smritikatha: Hemlata Tagore

Smritikatha: Dr Radhakamal Mukhopadhyay

Smritikatha: Musical genius Dilip Kumar Roy

Smritikatha: Rajarao Dhirendra Narayan Roy

Smritikatha: Soumendranath Tagore

Patra Patrika: Tattobodhini (1882-1898)

Patra Patrika: Bharati (1890-1900)

Patra Patrika: Balok (1883-1886)

Patra Patrika: Sanjibani (1881-1891) editor: Krishna Kumar Mitra

Patra Patrika: Prabasi (1892-1905)

Patra Patrika: Bangadarshan (1906-1910) editor: Rabindranath Tagore

Patra Patrika: Bichitra (variety editions)

Patra Patrika: Bharatbarsha (1911-1924)

Patra Patrika: Udbodhon 1902,1909,1911,1916,1936,1941)

Patra Patrika: Modern Review (1904, 1911 – 1913)

Patra Patrika: Spiritual Magazine (1902-1922)

Indian philosophical congress brochure number (1925)

Coolie: Ramkumar Bidyaratna

Himaronyo: Ramkumar Bidyaratna (Ramananda Bharati)

Tantriks and Tantrism: Dharmananda Bharati

Yogacharya Bhupendranath Sanyal: Centenary edition

The aim of Indian Life: Sister Nivedita

Master As I Saw Him: Sister Nivedita

Sri Ramkrishna Kathamrita (5th part) SriM

Vivekananda's quotes and writings: Swami Gyanatwananda

Swamiji's memory collection: Swami Nirlepananda

Karayogi Baherababa: Suprokash Bandyopadhaya and

Amitava Chakrabarti

Gyanganja: Mahamahopadhaya Doctor Gopinath Kabiraj

Sadhusanga and Satsanga (four parts) Doctor Gopinath Kabiraj

Srima Darshan (1-13 parts): Swami Nityananda

The Life Divine: Sri Arabinda

An Autobiography of a Yogi: Swami Yogananda

Sri Sri RamThakur Lila prasanga: Sri JibanTagore (Sri Ramnivas)

SriSri RamThakur (Centenary collection)

Veda Vani or Revelation Part III: Translated by Abani Mohan Banerjee

Haramoni (Md. Mansuruddin edited)

Brahma gayatri: jachak

The Spiritual Power That Wins: Swami R Ramthirtha

Secret Doctrine: Madam Blavatsky

Mahapith Tarapith (five parts): Bipul Kumar Gangopadhyay

Sadhu Sannidhe Sadhu Manishi: Bipul Kumar Gangopadhyay

Gita a Great Classic Contemplation: Dr Radhakamal Mukherjee

Key to the Kingdom of Health: Buddha Bose

Himalay: Jaladhar Sen

Himachalam: Rajarao Dhirenda Narayan Roy

Holy Kailash: Buddha Bose

Amritam Patrika: (1996-1999)

Sangeet Pad Kalpataru: Narendranath Dutta

Sri Sri Rangama's Life and quotes: Srimati Suchitra Tagore